# BIOLOGY

### THIRD EDITION

Ferguson's
*An Infobase Learning Company*

Careers in Focus: Biology

Ferguson's
An imprint of Infobase Learning
132 West 31st Street
New York NY 10001

Library of Congress Cataloging-in-Publication Data

Careers in focus. Biology. — 3rd ed.
    p. cm.
    Includes bibliographical references and index.
    ISBN-13: 978-0-8160-8030-4 (hardcover : alk. paper)
    ISBN-10: 0-8160-8030-5 (hardcover : alk. paper)   1. Biology—Vocational guidance—Juvenile literature.   I. Title: Biology.
    QH314.C37 2011
    570.23—dc22
                                                      2010044878

Ferguson's books are available at special discounts when purchased in bulk quantities for businesses, associations, institutions, or sales promotions. Please call our Special Sales Department in New York at (212) 967-8800 or (800) 322-8755.

You can find Ferguson's on the World Wide Web at
http://www.infobaselearning.com

Text design by David Strelecky
Composition by Newgen North America
Cover printed by Yurchak Printing, Landisville, Pa.
Book printed and bound by Yurchak Printing, Landisville, Pa.
Date printed: April 2011
Printed in the United States of America

10 9 8 7 6 5 4 3 2 1

This book is printed on acid-free paper.

All links and Web addresses were checked and verified to be correct at the time of publication. Because of the dynamic nature of the Web, some addresses and links may have changed since publication and may no longer be valid.

# Table of Contents

# Introduction

Life has many different levels of organization, from the atom to complex organisms to whole populations. The biological sciences look at life on one or more of these levels—at anything that is or has been alive. The field of biology also looks at the effects of surroundings on living things. People who study biology learn how living things work, how they relate to one another, and how they evolved. Studying biology teaches you to ask questions, judge evidence, and solve problems. Because living things vary greatly in how they live and where they came from, the field of biology is divided into many different specialty areas.

Biology subfields are many and varied and include microbiology, plant and animal physiology, ecology, epidemiology, cell biology, and oceanography, just to name a few. For all these areas, the elements of the job are essentially the same: building on the work of others, both past and present, through experimentation and observation.

Most research in biology uses a team approach. Team members review previous research and experiments and then set a goal for their project. They may either form a hypothesis (an educated guess) to prove or disprove a current theory, or they may set an open-ended objective, such as finding out what happens over time to people who smoke or drink. An experiment may prove something, or it may not. After experimentation, the biologist analyzes the results, often publishing his or her findings in a scientific journal article. Publishing results is a key part of doing research, for only by sharing data and evaluations can the scientific community make the most of research. Scientists working under contracts with research companies do not own their discoveries: Their research becomes the property of their employer. Scientists working independently can keep their discoveries as their own and have the right to patent and charge others for using their research.

Generally, those working in the biology field do one of four types of work: basic research, applied research, testing, or support. Basic research seeks knowledge for its own sake, uncovering fundamental truths and transforming the unknown into the known. Often done at universities, basic research includes all areas of biology. Applied research deals with translating basic knowledge into practical and useful products and processes for use in areas such as medicine or agriculture.

*Research biologists* at universities generally split their time between their research projects and teaching. *High school teachers* often specialize in biology and may teach courses that interest them personally, such as marine biology or physiology. Because researchers need skilled help from others trained in biology, some biologists work in support roles, such as laboratory technicians, who help carry out experiments. All specialists must combine a thorough knowledge of general biology with other skills and professional training.

Many people in the biology field do work that combines their knowledge of biology with other specialized training. The "office" for many of these jobs is the outdoors, and dress is casual. *Zookeepers*, for example, may work with captive breeding programs for endangered species. Zoos, museums, and nature centers hire educators, exhibit designers, artists, and other specialists with biology backgrounds. Those with a talent for writing may work as *science journalists*, breaking down science so that nonexperts can understand the concepts. Other biologists work as policy analysts in government, helping to develop science-based legislation. Physicians, dentists, nurses, medical technicians, and physician assistants must also have solid biology backgrounds.

Employment in the biological sciences is expected to grow much faster than the average for all careers through 2018, according to the U.S. Department of Labor. Genetics and biotechnology are two of the most promising employment areas for biologists. The American Institute of Biological Sciences says that plant geneticists, for example, will be needed to develop better methods of engineering crops. Researchers studying human biology will be hired in hopes of discovering ways to slow the aging process, cure genetic diseases, and reverse paralyzed nerve cells. Applications arising from new knowledge about recombinant DNA, or genetic engineering, promise to open up job opportunities, especially in the health care and pharmaceutical fields.

Biological scientists will also be needed to help study and protect wildlife, advise industry and politicians regarding environmental protection and pollutants, and develop biofuels.

However, biological scientists with Ph.D.'s may face stiff competition for research positions due to an increased number of doctorate-level biologists competing for the research grants. Although the federal government has substantially increased the amounts and kinds of grants available for biological research, only about one in four research proposals are approved for long-term studies, which reflects the strong competition in this field. Job opportunities for biologists with bachelor's and master's degrees will be better, as available positions in biology-related sales, marketing, education, and research management positions should be plentiful. The demand for biology-related technician positions in medicine and technology that do not require advanced degrees is also expected to be high. Continued and expanded research into diseases such as AIDS, cancer, and Alzheimer's and the need to develop new drugs and therapies to combat these diseases will also provide many opportunities for employment in the biology field.

Each article in *Careers in Focus: Biology* discusses a particular occupation in detail. The articles appear in Ferguson's *Encyclopedia of Careers and Vocational Guidance*, but they have been updated and revised with the latest information from the U.S. Department of Labor, professional organizations, and other sources. In addition, this revised edition of the book includes new articles on Astrobiologists, Biotechnology Patent Lawyers, Forensic Biologists, and Microbiologists. Each article is broken down in the following manner.

The **Quick Facts** section provides a brief summary of the career including recommended school subjects, personal skills, work environment, minimum educational requirements, salary ranges, certification or licensing requirements, and employment outlook. This section also provides acronyms and identification numbers for the following government classification indexes: the Dictionary of Occupational Titles (DOT), the Guide for Occupational Exploration (GOE), the National Occupational Classification (NOC) Index, and the Occupational Information Network (O*NET)-Standard Occupational Classification System (SOC) index. The DOT, GOE, and O*NET-SOC indexes have been created by the U.S. government; the NOC index is Canada's career classification system. Readers can use the identification numbers listed in the Quick Facts section to access further information about a career. Print editions of the DOT (*Dictionary of Occupational Titles.* Indianapolis, Ind.: JIST Works, 1991) and GOE (*Guide for Occupational Exploration.* Indianapolis, Ind.: JIST Works, 2001) are available at libraries. Electronic versions of the DOT (http://www.oalj.dol.gov/libdot.htm), NOC (http://www5.hrsdc.gc.ca/NOC), and O*NET-SOC (http://online.onetcenter.org) are available on the Internet. When no DOT, GOE, NOC, or O*NET-SOC numbers are listed, this means that the U.S. Department of Labor or Human Resources and Skills Development Canada have not created a numerical designation for this career. In this instance, you will see the acronym "N/A," or not available.

The **Overview** section is a brief introductory description of the duties and responsibilities involved in this career. Oftentimes, a career may have a variety of job titles. When this is the case, alternative career titles are presented. Employment statistics are also provided, when available. The **History** section describes the history of the particular job as it relates to the overall development of its industry or field. **The Job** describes the primary and secondary duties of the job. **Requirements** discusses high school and postsecondary education and training requirements, any certification or licensing that is necessary, and other personal requirements for success in the job. **Exploring** offers suggestions on how to gain experience in or knowledge of the particular job before making a firm educational and financial commitment. The focus is on what can be done while still in high school (or in the early years of college) to gain a better understanding of the job. The **Employers** section gives an overview of typical places of employment for the job. **Starting Out** discusses the best ways to land that first job, be it through the college career services office, newspaper ads, Internet employment sites, or personal contact. The **Advancement** section describes what kind of career path to expect from the job and how to get there. **Earnings** lists salary ranges and describes the typical fringe benefits. The **Work Environment** section describes the typical surroundings and conditions of employment—whether indoors or outdoors, noisy or quiet, social or independent. Also discussed are typical hours worked, any seasonal fluctuations, and the stresses and strains of the job. The **Outlook** section summarizes the job in terms of the general economy and industry projections. For the most part, Outlook information is obtained from the U.S. Bureau of Labor Statistics and is supplemented by information gathered from professional associations. Job growth terms follow those used in the *Occupational Outlook Handbook*. Growth described as "much faster than the average" means an increase of 20 percent or more. Growth described as "faster than the average" means an increase of 14 to 19 percent. Growth described as "about as fast as the average" means an increase of 7 to 13 percent. Growth described as "more slowly than the average" means an increase of 3 to 6 percent. "Little or no change" means a decrease of 2 percent to an increase of 2 percent. "Decline" means a decrease of 3 percent or more. Each article ends with **For More Information**, which lists organizations that provide information on training, education, internships, scholarships, and job placement.

*Careers in Focus: Biology* also includes photos, informative sidebars, and interviews with professionals in the field.

# Agricultural Scientists

## OVERVIEW

*Agricultural scientists* study all aspects of living organisms and the relationships of plants and animals to their environment. They conduct basic research in laboratories or in the field. They apply the results to such tasks as increasing crop yields and improving the environment. Some agricultural scientists plan and administer programs for testing foods, drugs, and other products. Others direct activities at public exhibits at such places as zoos and botanical gardens. Some agricultural scientists are professors at colleges and universities or work as consultants to business firms or the government. Others work in technical sales and service jobs for manufacturers of agricultural products. There are approximately 31,000 agricultural and food scientists in the United States.

## HISTORY

In 1840, Justius von Liebig of Germany published *Organic Chemistry in Its Applications to Agriculture and Physiology* and launched the systematic development of the agricultural sciences. A formal system of agricultural education soon followed in both Europe and the United States. Prior to the publication of this work, agricultural developments relied on the collective experience of farmers handed down over generations. Agricultural science has techniques in common with many other disciplines including biology, botany, genetics, nutrition, breeding, and engineering. Discoveries and improvements in these fields contributed to advances in agriculture. Some

### QUICK FACTS

**School Subjects**
Agriculture
Biology
Chemistry

**Personal Skills**
Communication/ideas
Technical/scientific

**Work Environment**
Indoors and outdoors
Primarily multiple locations

**Minimum Education Level**
Bachelor's degree

**Salary Range**
$34,930 to $59,180 to $107,670+

**Certification or Licensing**
Voluntary (certification)
Required for certain positions (licensing)

**Outlook**
Faster than the average

**DOT**
040, 041

**GOE**
02.02.02, 02.02.04

**NOC**
2121

**O*NET-SOC**
17-2021.00, 19-1012.00, 19-1013.00

A horticulturist inspects the size and quality of hydroponically grown strawberries. *(Ken Hammond, Agricultural Research Service, USDA)*

milestones include the discovery of the practice of crop rotation and the application of manure as fertilizer, which greatly increased farm yields in the 1700s. Farm mechanization was greatly advanced by the invention of the mechanical reaper in 1831 and the gasoline tractor in 1892. Chemical fertilizers were first used in the 19th century; pesticides and herbicides soon followed. In 1900, the research of an Austrian monk, Gregor Johann Mendel, was rediscovered. His theories of plant characteristics, based on studies using generations of garden peas, formed the foundation for the science of genetics.

In the 20th century, scientists and engineers were at the forefront of farm, crop, and food processing improvements. Conservationist Gifford Pinchot developed some of the first methods to prevent soil erosion in 1910, and Clarence Birdseye perfected a method of freezing food in the 1920s. Birdseye's discoveries allowed for new crops of produce previously too perishable for the marketplace. Engineers in the 1930s developed more powerful farm machinery and scientists developed hybrid corn. By the 1960s, high-powered machinery and better quality feed and pesticides were in common use. Today, advances in genetic engineering and biotechnology are leading to more efficient, economical methods of farming and new markets for crops.

Agricultural scientists are also playing an important role in the development of biofuels from renewable resources such as grasses, cow dung, leftover material from crops, and corn. In the past several years, researchers have found that growing corn as a biofuel can actually be harmful to the environment. Carol Werner, executive director of the Environmental and Energy Study Institute, says that the most environmentally friendly biofuels should be made from agricultural waste products (nonedible food products) and from biomass grown on nonagricultural lands.

Another fast-growing area is the use of nanotechnology in agricultural applications. Nanotechnology is a molecular manufacturing technology that is being used to test food and agricultural products to see if they are spoiled or contaminated.

## THE JOB

The nature of the work of the agricultural scientist can be broken down into several areas of specialization. Within each specialization there are various careers.

The following are careers that fall under the areas of plant and soil science.

*Agronomists* investigate large-scale food-crop problems, conduct experiments, and develop new methods of growing crops to ensure more efficient production, higher yields, and improved quality. They use genetic engineering to develop crops that are resistant to pests, drought, and plant diseases. They use biotechnology to increase the nutritional value of crops and the quality of seed stock.

Agronomists also engage in soil science. They analyze soils to find ways to increase production and reduce soil erosion. They study the responses of various soil types to fertilizers, tillage practices, and crop rotation. Since soil science is related to environmental science, agronomists may also use their expertise to consult with farmers and agricultural companies on environmental quality and effective land use.

*Botanists* are concerned with plants and their environment, structure, heredity, and economic value in such fields as agronomy, horticulture, and medicine. (See the article Botanists for more information.)

*Horticulturists* study fruit and nut orchards as well as garden plants such as vegetables and flowers. They conduct experiments to develop new and improved varieties and to increase crop quality and yields. They also work to improve plant culture methods for the landscaping and beautification of communities, parks, and homes.

*Plant breeders* apply genetics and biotechnology to improve plants' yield, quality, and resistance to harsh weather, disease, and insects. They might work on developing strains of wild or cultivated plants that will have a larger yield and increase profits.

*Plant pathologists* research plant diseases and the decay of plant products to identify symptoms, determine causes, and develop control measures. They attempt to predict outbreaks by studying how different soils, climates, and geography affect the spread and intensity of plant disease.

*Soil scientists* study the physical, chemical, and biological characteristics of soils to determine the most productive and effective planting strategies. Their research aids in producing larger, healthier crops and more environmentally sound farming procedures.

Another area of specialization for agricultural scientists is animal science.

*Animal scientists* conduct research and develop improved methods for housing, breeding, feeding, and controlling diseases of domestic farm animals. They inspect and grade livestock food products, purchase livestock, or work in sales and marketing of livestock products. They often consult agricultural businesses on such areas as upgrading animal housing, lowering mortality rates, or increasing production of animal products such as milk and eggs.

*Dairy scientists* study the selection, breeding, feeding, and management of dairy cattle. For example, they research how various types of food and environmental conditions affect milk production and quality. They also develop new breeding programs to improve dairy herds.

*Poultry scientists* study the breeding, feeding, and management of poultry to improve the quantity and quality of eggs and other poultry products.

*Animal breeders* specialize in improving the quality of farm animals. They may work for a state agricultural department, agricultural extension station, or university. Some of their work is done in a laboratory, but much of it is done outdoors working directly on animals. Using their knowledge of genetics, animal breeders develop systems for animals to achieve desired characteristics such as strength, fast maturation, resistance to disease, and quality of meat.

Food science is a specialty closely related to animal science, but it focuses on meeting consumer demand for food products in ways that are healthy, safe, and convenient.

*Food scientists* use their backgrounds in chemistry, microbiology, and other sciences to develop new or better ways of preserving, packaging, processing, storing, and delivering foods. *Food technologists* work in product development to discover new food sources and analyze food content to determine levels of vitamins, fat, sugar, and protein. Food technologists also work to enforce government regulations, inspecting food processing areas and ensuring that sanitation, safety, quality, and waste management standards are met.

Another field related to agricultural science is agricultural engineering.

*Agricultural engineers* apply engineering principles to work in the food and agriculture industries. They design or develop agricultural equipment and machines, supervise production, and conduct tests on new designs and machine parts. They develop plans and specifications for agricultural buildings and for drainage and irrigation systems. They work on flood control, soil erosion, and land reclamation projects. They design food processing systems and equipment to convert farm products to consumer foods. Agricultural engineers contribute to making farming easier and more profitable through the introduction of new farm machinery and through advancements in soil and water conservation. Agricultural engineers in industry engage in research or in the design, testing, or sales of equipment.

Much of the research conducted by agricultural scientists is done in laboratories and requires a familiarity with research techniques and the use of laboratory equipment and computers. Some research, however, is carried out wherever necessary. A botanist may have occasion to examine the plants that grow in the volcanic valleys of Alaska, or an animal breeder may study the behavior of animals on the plains of Africa.

# REQUIREMENTS

## High School

Follow your high school's college preparatory program, which will include courses in English, foreign language, mathematics, and government. Also take biology, chemistry, physics, and any other science courses available. You must also become familiar with basic computer skills, including programming. It may be possible for you to perform laboratory assistant duties for your science teachers. Visiting research laboratories and attending lectures by agricultural scientists can also be helpful.

## Postsecondary Training

Educational requirements for agricultural scientists are very high. A master's degree, or more often a doctorate, is usually mandatory for careers as college or university professors, independent researchers, or field managers. A bachelor's degree may be acceptable for some entry-level jobs, such as testing or inspecting technicians, or as technical sales or service representatives. Promotions, however, are very limited for these employees unless they earn advanced degrees.

To become an agricultural scientist, you should pursue a degree related to agricultural and biological science. As an undergraduate, you should have a firm foundation in biology, with courses in chemistry, physics, mathematics, and English. Most colleges and universities have agricultural science curriculums, although liberal arts colleges may emphasize the biological sciences. State universities usually offer agricultural science programs, too.

While pursuing an advanced degree, you'll participate in research projects and write a dissertation on your specialized area of study. You'll also do fieldwork and laboratory research along with your classroom studies.

## Certification or Licensing

The American Society of Agronomy and the Soil Science Society of America offer several certifications—including the certified crop adviser, certified professional agronomist, and certified professional soil scientist/classifier designations—to candidates based on their training and work. Contact the organizations for more information.

According to the American Society of Agricultural Engineers, agricultural engineers must hold an engineer's license.

## Other Requirements

As a researcher, you should be self-motivated enough to work effectively alone, yet be able to function cooperatively as part of a team.

You should have an inexhaustible curiosity about the nature of living things and their environments. You must be systematic in your work habits and in your approach to investigation and experimentation and must have the persistence to continue or start over when experiments are not immediately successful.

Work performed by agricultural scientists in offices and laboratories requires intense powers of concentration and the ability to communicate one's thoughts systematically. In addition to these skills, physical stamina is necessary for those scientists who do field research in remote areas of the world.

## EXPLORING

If you live in an agricultural community, you may be able to find part-time or summer work on a farm or ranch. Joining a chapter of the National FFA Organization (formerly Future Farmers of America) or a 4-H program will introduce you to the concerns of farmers and researchers and may involve you directly in science projects. Contact your county's extension office to learn about regional projects. You may also find part-time work in veterinarian's offices, florist shops, landscape nurseries, orchards, farms, zoos, aquariums, botanical gardens, or museums. Volunteer work is often available in zoos and animal shelters.

## EMPLOYERS

There are approximately 31,000 agricultural and food scientists employed in the United States. About 20 percent are employed by manufacturing companies—mainly in food and pharmaceutical manufacturing. Another 15 percent work in educational institutions. Scientists with doctorates may work on the faculty of colleges and universities. About 7 percent of all agricultural and food scientists work for the federal government. They work within the U.S. Department of Agriculture and the Environmental Protection Agency and for regional extension agencies and soil conservation departments.

## STARTING OUT

Agricultural scientists often are recruited prior to graduation. College and university career services offices offer information about jobs, and students may arrange interviews with recruiters who visit the campus.

Direct application may be made to the personnel departments of colleges and universities, private industries, and nonprofit research foundations. People interested in positions with the federal government may contact the local offices of state employment services and the U.S. Office of Personnel Management (http://www.usajobs.opm.gov), which are located in various large cities throughout the country. Private employment agencies are another method that might be considered. Large companies sometimes conduct job fairs in major cities and will advertise them in the business sections of the local newspapers.

## ADVANCEMENT

Advancement in this field depends on education, experience, and job performance. Agricultural scientists with advanced degrees generally start in teaching or research and advance to administrative and management positions, such as supervisor of a research program. The number of such jobs is limited, however, and often the route to advancement is through specialization. The narrower specialties are often the most valuable.

People who enter this field with only a bachelor's degree are much more restricted. After starting in testing and inspecting jobs or as technical sales and service representatives, they may progress to advanced technicians, particularly in medical research, or become high school biology teachers. In the latter case, they must have had courses in education and meet the state requirements for teaching credentials.

## EARNINGS

According to the U.S. Department of Labor (DOL), the median annual salary of soil and plant scientists was approximately $59,180 in 2009. The lowest paid 10 percent (which generally included those just starting out in the field) earned less than $34,930, while the highest paid 10 percent made approximately $107,670 or more per year. Unless hired for just a short-term project, agricultural scientists most likely receive health and retirement benefits in addition to their annual salary.

## WORK ENVIRONMENT

Agricultural scientists work regular hours, although researchers often choose to work longer when their experiments have reached critical points. Competition in the research field may be stiff, causing a certain amount of stress.

Agricultural scientists generally work in offices, laboratories, or classrooms where the environment is clean, healthy, and safe. Some agricultural scientists, such as botanists, periodically take field trips where living facilities may be primitive and strenuous physical activity may be required.

## OUTLOOK

According to the DOL, employment for agricultural scientists is expected to grow faster than the average for all occupations through 2018. The fields of biotechnology, nanotechnology, biosecurity, genetics, and sustainable agriculture will hold the best opportunities for agricultural scientists. New developments, such as methods of processing corn and other crops for use in medicines and for fuel for motor vehicles, will alter the marketplace. Scientists will also be actively involved in improving both the environmental impact of farming and crop yields, as they focus on methods of decontaminating soil, protecting groundwater, crop rotation, and other efforts of conservation. Scientists will also have the challenge of promoting these new methods to farmers. Employment growth for animal scientists should be slightly slower than that of soil and plant scientists and food scientists and technologists.

## FOR MORE INFORMATION

*To learn about opportunities for scientists in the dairy industry and for information on student divisions at the college level, visit the association's Web site.*
American Dairy Science Association
2441 Village Green Place
Champaign, IL 61822-7676
Tel: 217-356-5146
E-mail: adsa@assochq.org
http://www.adsa.org

*To learn about careers and student competitions and scholarships, contact*
American Society of Agricultural and Biological Engineers
2950 Niles Road
St. Joseph, MI 49085-8607
Tel: 269-429-0300
E-mail: hq@asabe.org
http://www.asabe.org

*For information on careers and certification, contact*
**American Society of Agronomy**
5585 Guilford Road
Madison, WI 53711-5801
Tel: 608-273-8080
https://www.agronomy.org

*For information on careers, contact*
**Crop Science Society of America**
5585 Guilford Road
Madison, WI 53711-5801
https://www.crops.org

*For information on accredited food science programs and careers,*
*visit the IFT Web site.*
**Institute of Food Technologists (IFT)**
525 West Van Buren, Suite 1000
Chicago, IL 60607-3830
Tel: 312-782-8424
E-mail: info@ift.org
http://www.ift.org

*For more information on agricultural careers and student programs,*
*contact*
**National FFA Organization**
6060 FFA Drive
PO Box 68960
Indianapolis, IN 46268-0960
Tel: 317-802-6060
http://www.ffa.org

*For industry news and updates and general information on bio-*
*energy, contact*
**Renewable Fuels Association**
425 Third Street, SW, Suite 1150
Washington, DC 20024-3231
Tel: 202-289-3835
http://www.ethanolrfa.org

*For information on certification and the career brochure* Soils
Sustain Life, *contact*
**Soil Science Society of America**
5585 Guilford Road
Madison, WI 53711-5801

Tel: 608-273-8080
https://www.soils.org

*Visit the USDA Web site for more information on its agencies and programs as well as news releases.*
United States Department of Agriculture (USDA)
1400 Independence Avenue, SW
Washington, DC 20250-0002
Tel: 202-720-2791
http://www.usda.gov

## —— INTERVIEW ——

*Carolyn M. Jones, P.E., is an agricultural engineer for the U.S. Department of Agriculture's Natural Resources Conservation Service in Napa County, California. She discussed her career with the editors of* Careers in Focus: Biology.

**Q. How long have you worked in the field? What made you want to become an agricultural engineer?**

**A.** I've been working with the Natural Resources Conservation Service (NRCS) since 2000 when I did an internship during college in the Solano County Field Office. I spent 4.5 years after graduation working out of our state office in Davis, where I helped out a number of offices around the state with designs, surveying, and quick answers to technical questions. When I was in high school, I was both enrolled in honors science and math courses and actively involved in my FFA chapter and my vocational agriculture classes. Wanting to combine my interest in math and science with work in agriculture, I pursued agricultural engineering when I was admitted to the University of California–Davis.

**Q. What is one thing that young people may not know about a career in agricultural engineering?**

**A.** Agricultural engineering is about more than wanting to farm well. It's about applying ingenuity and science to the farm, farming activities, the effects of farming activities, farming structures and infrastructure, and farming products that range from tomatoes to bananas, green beans to peanuts, wine grapes to corn for biodiesel, trees for lumber to cotton, or fish to cattle. My colleagues design things ranging from tractors and harvesters, to barns and greenhouses, to bioreactors and manure digesters, to irrigation systems, veterinary devices, and bioenergy systems. Additionally, all fields of engineering are about protecting the public—people, wildlife, and the environment.

**Q. Can you please briefly describe a day in your life on the job?**

**A.** A typical day at my job varies nicely. Some days are spent talking with landowners, potential clients, about the goals they have for their land and how we may be able to help them or attending meetings to either inform people or support the balance of agricultural and environmental goals. A typical "engineering" day might consist of a morning spent creating a topographic survey of a project area and an afternoon working with that survey in a computer drafting program quantifying design elements, calculating design parameters, and preparing construction drawings that are part of the landowner's design docket. And I regularly need to talk to my colleagues about how my engineering work interfaces with the soil, plant, and animal resources in the system. Many summer days are spent in the field inspecting and monitoring the construction of projects designed the prior winter.

**Q. How did you train for this job? What was your college major?**

**A.** I earned a college degree in biosystems and agricultural engineering with an emphasis in agricultural engineering and have since become licensed in both agricultural and civil engineering. Honestly, my early training for what I do now began when I was learning hands-on, vocational agriculture through 4-H, FFA, and work at home and in the outdoors. It was that hands-on experience that—paired with the math and science that I learned in high school and college—have helped me design practical solutions. A major part of what I know and apply on the job daily comes from more specialized training that I've gained on the job from colleagues and practice and from short courses since college.

**Q. What are the most important personal and professional qualities for agricultural engineers?**

**A.** Important personal and professional qualities for agricultural engineers, and engineers in general, are to 1) listen to the owner's goals; 2) be sure you convey your thoughts clearly whether written, drawn, or spoken (yes, engineers have to know how to write well); 3) be an advocate for the public, which includes the farm and the environment; 4) listen to the ideas of others, including the contractors that have been in construction for longer than you've been an engineer; 5) know when to put your foot down and when another option might work; 6) budget time and know the timeline for a project; 7) show off your achievements (in the right forum, of course); 8) take opportunities to teach others what you know; 9) stop and enjoy what you're doing and where you are now and then; 10) document your progress, your questions, your decisions, your successes, and your failures; 11) keep yourself organized and prepared; 12) acknowledge when you need help; 13) maintain a life outside of work; 14) keep learning and don't be afraid to admit what you don't know because people will appreciate your honesty; 15) maintain a sense of humor; and 16) know when to end a list.

**Q. What advice would you give to young people who are interested in the field?**
**A.** My best advice for anyone interested in agricultural engineering is to contact someone in the field and ask for an internship or a chance to volunteer with their organization or company.

# Aquarists

## OVERVIEW

*Aquarists* (pronounced, like "aquarium," with the accent on the second syllable) work for aquariums, oceanariums, and marine research institutes. They maintain aquatic exhibits. Among other duties, they feed the fish, check water quality, clean the tanks, and collect and transport new specimens.

## HISTORY

In 1853, the world's first public aquarium opened in Regents Park in London. Similar public aquariums opened throughout England, France, and Germany over the next 15 years. Many of the early aquariums closed because the fish could not survive in the conditions provided. By the early 1870s, knowledge of aeration, filtering, and water temperature had increased, and new aquariums opened.

In 1856, the U.S. government established what is today the Division of Fishes of the Smithsonian Institution's National Museum of Natural History. Over the next 50 years interest in fish and their environments grew rapidly. The Scripps Institution of Oceanography was established in 1903, and the Woods Hole Oceanographic Institute was established in 1930.

Today's notable aquariums include the John G. Shedd Aquarium, Chicago; the National Aquarium, Baltimore; the Georgia Aquarium, Atlanta, Georgia; the New York Aquarium, New York City; the Steinhart Aquarium, San Francisco; and the Audubon Aquarium of the Americas, New Orleans. Many aquariums re-create diverse aquatic environments, such as coral reefs, river bottoms, or various coastlines, in large tanks.

An aquarist (*left*) and his assistant lift a zebra shark out of the water for examination at the PPG Aquarium in Pittsburgh, Pennsylvania. *(Steve Adams, The Tribune-Review/AP Photo)*

Some aquariums also have oceanariums—huge tanks that allow visitors to view marine animals from above as well as from the sides. Popular oceanariums include those at the Miami Seaquarium in Miami, Florida, and the Monterey Bay Aquarium in Monterey, California.

## THE JOB

Aquarists work for aquariums, oceanariums, and marine research institutes. Aquarists are not animal trainers and do not work on marine shows. They do, however, support the staff who do. Their work is generally technical and requires a strong science background. With increased experience and education, aquarists may, in time, become involved in research efforts at their institution or become promoted to higher professional positions such as curator.

Aquarists' job duties are similar to those of zookeepers. Aquarists feed fish and other marine animals, maintain exhibits, and conduct research. They work on breeding, conservation, and educational programs.

Aquarists clean and take care of tanks every day. They make sure pumps are working, check water temperatures, clean glass, and sift sand. Some exhibits have to be scrubbed by hand. Aquarists also change the water and vacuum tanks routinely. They water plants in marsh or pond exhibits.

Food preparation and feeding are important tasks for aquarists. Some animals eat live food and others eat cut-up food mixtures. Some animals need special diets prepared and may have to be individually fed.

Aquarists carefully observe all the animals in their care. They must understand their normal habits (including mating, feeding, sleeping, and moving) in order to be able to judge when something is wrong. Aquarists write daily reports and keep detailed records of animal behavior.

Many aquarists are in charge of collecting and stocking plants and animals for exhibits. They may have to make several trips a year to gather live specimens.

## REQUIREMENTS

### High School

If you want to become an aquarist, get your start in high school. Take as many science classes as you can; biology and zoology are especially important. Learn to pay attention to detail as marine science involves a good deal of careful record keeping.

### Postsecondary Training

Most aquariums, along with other institutions that hire aquarists, require that an applicant have a bachelor's degree in biological sciences, preferably with course work in such areas as parasitology (the study of parasites and their hosts), ichthyology (the study of fishes), or other aquatic sciences. As the care of captive animals becomes a more complex discipline, it's no longer enough to apply without a four-year degree.

### Certification or Licensing

Aquarists must be able to dive, in both contained water, to feed fish and maintain tanks, and in open water, on trips to collect new specimens. You'll need to have scuba certification, with a rescue diver classification, for this job. Organizations such as PADI provide basic certification. Potential employers will expect you to be able to pass a diving physical examination before taking you on as an aquarist. You may also need to have a special collector's permit from the state in which you work that allows you to gather samples for your aquarium.

### Other Requirements

As an aquarist, you may be required to travel at different times throughout the year, to participate in research expeditions and collecting trips. On a more basic level, aquarists need to be in good physical shape, with good hearing and visual acuity. Some employers also require a certain strength level—say, the ability to regularly exert 100 pounds of force—since equipment, feed, and the animals themselves can be heavy and often unwieldy. Good communication and teamwork skills are also important.

## EXPLORING

In addition to formal education, many aquariums, like other types of museums, look for a strong interest in the field before hiring an applicant. Most often, they look for a history of volunteering. That means you need to look for every avenue you can find to work around fish or other animals. Do as much as your schedule allows. Even working part time or volunteering at a local pet store counts. Also, be sure to ask your career guidance counselor for information on marine science careers and opportunities for summer internships or college scholarships offered by larger institutes.

You should also consider joining the Association of Zoos and Aquariums (AZA), which offers an associate membership category "for zoo and aquarium professionals, as well as other interested parties, who want to support and forward the mission, vision, and goals of AZA."

## EMPLOYERS

Aquarists most often work in zoos, public aquariums, or in research jobs with marine science institutes.

## STARTING OUT

Full-time jobs for aquarists can be scarce, especially for those just starting in the field. Part-time or volunteer positions with zoos, aquariums, science institutes, nature centers, or even pet stores could provide valuable preliminary experience that may eventually lead to a full-time position.

## ADVANCEMENT

The usual career path for an aquarist progresses from intern/volunteer through part-time work to full-fledged aquarist, senior aquarist, supervisor, and finally, curator. Each step along the path requires additional experience and often additional education. Curators generally are expected to have a Ph.D. in a relevant marine science discipline, for example. The career path of an aquarist depends on how much hands-on work they like to do with animals. Other options are available for aquarists who are looking for a less "down and dirty" experience.

## EARNINGS

Aquariums often are nonprofit institutions, limiting the earnings ability in this job somewhat. In general, aquarists make between $22,000 and $41,600 a year. Salaries for nonfarm animal caretakers (a career category that includes aquarists) ranged from less than $15,590 to $31,660 or more in 2009, according to the U.S. Department of Labor.

Aquariums offer fairly extensive benefits, including health insurance, 401(k) plans, continuing education opportunities, tuition reimbursement, and reciprocal benefits with many other cultural institutions.

## WORK ENVIRONMENT

Aquarists may work indoors or outdoors, depending on the facility for which they work and the exhibit to which they're assigned. Aquarists spend a lot of time in the water. Their day will be filled with a variety of tasks, some repetitive, like feeding, others unusual, such as working with rescued marine mammals, perhaps. In the beginning, aquarists work under the supervision of a senior aquarist or supervisor and may work as part of a team. Aquarists also can expect to travel as part of the job.

## OUTLOOK

There is, in general, little change in the availability of positions for aquarists. While terrestrial zoos have begun to add aquarium complexes to their campuses in growing numbers, an actual boom in the construction of new aquariums is unlikely at this time. Many aquarists do advance to other positions, however, so openings do become available. Aquarists with advanced degrees and training who are willing to relocate will have the best employment opportunities.

## FOR MORE INFORMATION

*Visit the alliance's Web site for information on marine mammals, internships, and publications.*

**Alliance of Marine Mammal Parks and Aquariums**
E-mail: ammpa@aol.com
http://www.ammpa.org

*For information on membership, a list of accredited zoos through-
out the world, and careers in aquatic and marine science, including
job listings, contact*
**Association of Zoos and Aquariums**
8403 Colesville Road, Suite 710
Silver Spring, MD 20910-3314
Tel: 301-562-0777
http://www.aza.org

*For information on diving instruction and certification, contact*
**PADI**
30151 Tomas Street
Rancho Santa Margarita, CA 92688-2125
Tel: 800-729-7234
http://www.padi.com

# Astrobiologists

## QUICK FACTS

**School Subjects**
Biology
Physiology

**Personal Skills**
Mechanical/manipulative
Technical/scientific

**Work Environment**
Indoors and outdoors
Primarily multiple locations

**Minimum Education Level**
Bachelor's degree

**Salary Range**
$36,750 to $66,510 to
$100,580+

**Certification or Licensing**
None available

**Outlook**
About as fast as the average

**DOT**
041

**GOE**
02.03.03

**NOC**
2121

**O*NET-SOC**
19-1021.00, 19-1022.00,
19-1023.00, 19-1029.00

## OVERVIEW

*Astrobiologists*, also known as *exobiologists, life scientists*, and *space scientists*, study the origin of all life forms, from a simple one-celled organism, to plants, to human beings. They study and research the evolution, distribution, and future of these life forms, on earth as well as on other planets in our solar system and beyond. Many astrobiologists are employed by the National Aeronautics and Space Administration (NASA) and other government funded agencies. They are also employed at private research institutions and colleges and universities.

## HISTORY

Throughout the course of history, humans have been interested in science. Taxonomy, the science of classifying living things, was practiced whenever farmers chose to plant certain seeds they found superior to others. Ecology, the study of living things in relation to their environment, was practiced as farmers learned to rotate their crops in order to better take care of the soil and produce strong crop yields. Simple principles of genetics, the science of genes and heredity, was applied by Gregor Mendel during his crossbreeding experiments. Many more scientists and inventors through the centuries have used the principles of chemistry, physics, biology, and mathematics, to help understand the history of people, animals, and plants, as well as help improve the quality of everyday life.

Astrobiology, the study of the origin, development, and distribution of all forms of life, grew from many different specialties of life and earth science. Its name is derived from the Greek words *astron* (star), *bios* (life), and *logos* (science). As astrobiologists seek to find how life began and is affected by evolution and environment, they use the ideas, techniques, and philosophy of such sciences as geology, astronomy, chemistry, microbiology, molecular biology, biogeochemistry, and oceanography. They use the same concepts to study whether life exists on other planets. In fact, most astrobiologists receive their early education and training in other sciences, before specializing in the field of astrobiology.

Only a few universities in the United States offer graduate programs in astrobiology. One of these, the University of Washington, offers the only doctoral program geared to find and study life in outer space. Private research institutes, such as the SETI Institute, employs astrobiologists to staff research projects such as understanding the biosphere of Mars or how perennial hot springs exist in the Canadian Arctic. Many astrobiologists work at NASA's research institutes, including the Ames Research Center in California.

In 1995, NASA organized the NASA Astrobiology Institute (NAI) a partnership between the government agency, academic institutes, and research centers throughout the United States. Today, about 700 scientists, researchers, and educators work together at the NAI to learn more about the living universe.

## THE JOB

Astrobiologists study the origin, evolution, distribution, and future of all life forms in the universe. Astrobiologists' work is varied; they try to find answers to such questions as how life forms are affected by changes in environment, if any forms of life exist on other planets, as well as the adaptability of human beings to extraterrestrial environments.

Most astrobiologists work for government-funded agencies such as NASA. For example, at NASA's Ames Research Center, astrobiologists could be assigned to work on research projects covering animal muscle evolution or plant adaptation. Much of their work takes place inside a laboratory with actual specimens, but sometimes the nature of their research takes them to different places around the world. Some are even assigned to help plan and monitor experiments for future spaceflight missions.

Many other astrobiologists find work at the university level, either as researchers or educators. Academic positions are quite competitive, since only a few schools offer programs devoted to astrobiology. However, this may change in the near future as interest grows in this interdisciplinary field.

Astrobiologists also work at private research institutes located worldwide. An astrobiologist employed as a researcher at the Scripps Research Institute, for example, might conduct studies on the effects of drastic environments on simple proteins. Researchers strive to have their work published in industry journals such as *Astrobiology Magazine* or presented at seminars offered by the NAI.

## REQUIREMENTS

### High School
Are you signed up for freshman year earth science? This and related courses will provide you with a solid foundation for your future career. Other classes to consider are biology, chemistry, physics, geology, botany, and mathematics. Also consider nonscience courses such as speech and English, or any classes that can sharpen your communication skills. What's the point of knowing everything there is to know about algae or hydrothermal springs if you can't convey your ideas to others?

### Postsecondary Training
Astrobiology is an interdisciplinary science, and as such, scientists, researchers, and educators working in this field come from a variety of educational backgrounds, with undergraduate degrees ranging from biology to chemistry to astronomy. Some astrobiologists, especially those doing laboratory work, may find employment with a bachelor's degree. However, the majority of top researchers, and certainly those teaching at universities, have earned or are in the process of completing their Ph.D.'s. A small number of universities, such as the University of California–Los Angeles (http://www .ess.ucla.edu/research/astrobio.asp), the University of Washington (http://depts.washington.edu/astrobio), Arizona State University (http://astrobiology.asu.edu), and the University of Colorado (http:// lasp.colorado.edu/life) offer graduate programs or coursework in astrobiology. Also, annual conferences for astrobiology graduate students, such as the one held by Arizona State University, can provide information on new programs starting at other universities.

### Other Requirements
Astrobiologists must be systematic in their approach to solving problems. They should have probing, inquisitive minds and an aptitude for biology, geology, chemistry, astronomy, microbiology, molecular biology, biogeochemistry, oceanography, and mathematics. Patience and imagination are also required, since they may spend much time in observation and analysis. Astrobiologists must also have good

communication skills in order to gather and exchange data and solve problems that arise in their work.

## EXPLORING

Students can measure their aptitude and interest in the work of the astrobiologist by taking biology courses. Laboratory assignments, for example, provide information on techniques used by the working astrobiologist. Many schools hire students as laboratory assistants to work directly under a teacher and help administer the laboratory sections of courses.

School assemblies, field trips to federal and private laboratories and research centers, and career conferences provide additional insight into career opportunities. Advanced students often are able to attend professional meetings and seminars.

Part-time and summer positions in biology or related areas are particularly helpful. Students with some college courses in biology and astrobiology may find summer positions as laboratory assistants. Graduate students may find work on research projects conducted by their institutions. Beginning college and advanced high school students may find employment as laboratory aides or hospital orderlies or attendants. Despite the menial nature of these positions, they afford a useful insight into careers in biology and astrobiology. High school students often have the opportunity to join volunteer service groups at local hospitals. Student science training programs at colleges and universities allow qualified high school students to spend a summer doing research under the supervision of a scientist.

## EMPLOYERS

About 40 percent of all biological scientists work for the government at the federal, state, or local level. Astrobiologists are employed by the National Aeronautics and Space Administration and other government funded agencies. They also work at private research institutions and colleges and universities.

## STARTING OUT

Students interested in becoming teachers should consult their college's career services office. An increasing number of colleges hire teachers through the colleges at which they studied. Some teaching positions are filled through direct application.

Astrobiologists interested in private industry and nonprofit organizations may also apply directly for employment. Major organizations, such as NASA, that employ astrobiologists often interview college seniors on campus. Private and public employment offices frequently have listings from these employers. Experienced astrobiologists may change positions as a result of contacts made at professional seminars and national conventions.

Special application procedures are required for positions with government agencies. Civil service applications for federal, state, and municipal positions may be obtained by contacting the agency involved and from high school and college guidance and placement bureaus, public employment agencies, and post offices.

## ADVANCEMENT

To a great extent, advancement for astrobiologists depends on the individual's level of education. A doctorate is generally required for college teaching, independent research, and top-level administrative and management jobs. A master's degree is sufficient for some jobs in applied research, and a bachelor's degree may qualify for some entry-level jobs.

With the right qualifications, an astrobiologist may advance to the position of project chief and direct a team of other astrobiologists. Many use their knowledge and experience as background for administrative and management positions. Often, as they develop professional expertise, astrobiologists move from strictly technical assignments into positions in which they interpret astrobiological knowledge.

## EARNINGS

Earnings for astrobiologists vary extensively based on the type and size of their employer and the individual's level of education and experience. The U.S. Department of Labor (DOL) does not provide salary information for astrobiologists, but it does report that the median salary for all biological scientists was $66,510 in 2009. Salaries ranged from less than $36,750 to more than $100,580. In 2009, general biological scientists working for the federal government earned a mean salary of $73,030. Scientists employed by NASA earned starting salaries that ranged from $33,151 to $44,034 in 2010.

Astrobiologists are usually eligible for health and dental insurance, paid vacations and sick days, and retirement plans. Some employers may offer reimbursement for continuing education, seminars, and travel.

## WORK ENVIRONMENT

The astrobiologist's work environment varies greatly, depending upon the position and type of employer. One astrobiologist may work outdoors or travel much of the time. Another may wear a white smock and spend years working in a laboratory. Some work with toxic substances and disease cultures; strict safety measures must be observed.

## OUTLOOK

The DOL predicts that employment for all biological scientists will grow much faster than the average for all careers through 2018. Despite this prediction, it is important to remember that astrobiology is still a very small field. Competition will be stiff for top positions. For example, Ph.D.'s looking for research positions will find strong competition for a limited number of openings. In addition, certain government jobs as well as government funding for research may also be less plentiful. A recession or shift in political power can cause the loss of funding for grants and the decline of research and development endeavors.

Astrobiologists with advanced degrees will be best qualified for the most lucrative and challenging jobs. Scientists with bachelor's degrees may find openings as science or engineering technicians or as health technologists and technicians.

## FOR MORE INFORMATION

*For information on careers in biology, contact*
**American Institute of Biological Sciences**
1444 I Street, NW, Suite 200
Washington, DC 20005-6535
Tel: 202-628-1500
E-mail: admin@aibs.org
http://www.aibs.org

*For a career brochure, career-related articles, and a list of institutions that award academic degrees with a major in physiology, contact*
**American Physiological Society**
9650 Rockville Pike
Bethesda, MD 20814-3991
Tel: 301-634-7164
http://www.the-aps.org

*For information on careers, educational resources, and fellowships, contact*
**American Society for Microbiology**
1752 N Street, NW
Washington, DC 20036-2904
Tel: 202-737-3600
http://www.asm.org

*The NASA Astrobiology Institute is focused on the xenobiologic study of the living universe. For information on its current research projects, fellowships, and other educational opportunities, contact*
**NASA Astrobiology Institute**
Tel: 650-604-0809
http://astrobiology.nasa.gov/nai

*The Scripps Research Institute is the largest private, nonprofit research organization in the United States. Its research is biomedically focused. To learn more about the institute's research projects currently in progress at its California or Florida facilities, or to obtain information regarding the doctorate program, contact*
**Scripps Research Institute**
10550 North Torrey Pines Road
La Jolla, CA 92037-1000
Tel: 858-784-1000
http://www.scripps.edu

*This magazine features monthly "hot topics" ranging from extrasolar life to terrestrial origins. Its online version also offers a forum, a collection of astrobiology images, and news of the latest advancements in the field of astrobiology.*
***Astrobiology***
http://www.astrobio.net

*Visit the following Web site to learn more about exobiology:*
**Exobiology: Life Through Space and Time**
http://exobiology.arc.nasa.gov

# Biochemists

## OVERVIEW

*Biochemists* explore the tiny world of the cell, study how illnesses develop, and search for ways to improve life on earth. Through studying the chemical makeup of living organisms, biochemists strive to understand the dynamics of life, from the secrets of cell-to-cell communication to the chemical changes in our brains that give us memories. Biochemists examine the chemical combinations and reactions involved in such functions as growth, metabolism, reproduction, and heredity. They also study the effect of environment on living tissue. If cancer is to be cured, the earth's pollution cleaned up, or the aging process slowed, it will be biochemists and molecular biologists who will lead the way. There are approximately 23,200 biochemists and biophysicists employed in the United States. (*Biophysicists* examine the chemical combinations and reactions involved in such functions as metabolism and heredity.)

## HISTORY

Biochemistry is a fairly new science, even though the concept of biochemistry is said to have its roots in the discovery of the fermentation process thousands of years ago. In fact, the basic steps used to make wine from grapes were the same in ancient times as they are today. However, the rather unchanging methods used for alcohol fermentation do not nearly reflect the revolutionary changes that have occurred throughout recent history in our knowledge of cell composition, growth, and function.

Robert Hooke, an English scientist, first described and named cells in 1665, when he looked at a slice of bark from an oak tree under a

## QUICK FACTS

**School Subjects**
Biology
Chemistry

**Personal Skills**
Mechanical/manipulative
Technical/scientific

**Work Environment**
Primarily indoors
Primarily one location

**Minimum Education Level**
Bachelor's degree

**Salary Range**
$33,254 to $82,390 to
$138,820+

**Certification or Licensing**
Required for certain positions

**Outlook**
Much faster than the average

**DOT**
041

**GOE**
02.03.03

**NOC**
2112

**O*NET-SOC**
19-1021.00, 19-1021.01

microscope with a magnifying power of 30x. Hooke never realized the significance of his discovery, however, because he thought the tiny boxes or "cells" he saw were unique to the bark. Anton van Leeuwenhoek, a Dutchman who lived in Hooke's time, discovered the existence of single-celled organisms by observing them in pond water and in animal blood and sperm. He used grains of sand that he had polished into magnifying glasses as powerful as 300x to see this invisible world. In 1839, nearly two centuries after Hooke's and Leeuwenhoek's discoveries, two German biologists, Matthias Schleiden and Theodor Schwann, correctly concluded that all living things consisted of cells. This theory was later expanded to include the idea that all cells come from other cells, and that the ability of cells to divide to form new cells is the basis for all reproduction, growth, and repair of many-celled organisms, like humans.

Over the past decades, a powerful instrument called the electron microscope has revealed the complex structure of cells. Every cell, at some state in its life, contains deoxyribonucleic acid, or DNA, the genetic material that directs the cell's many activities. Biochemists have widened their scope to include the study of protein molecules and chromosomes, the building blocks of life itself. Biology and chemistry have always been allied sciences, and the exploration of cells and their molecular components, carried out by biochemists and other biological scientists, has revealed much about life. James Watson's and Francis Crick's breakthrough discovery of the structure of DNA in 1953 touched off a flurry of scientific activity that led to a better and better understanding of DNA chemistry and the genetic code. These discoveries eventually made it possible to manipulate DNA, enabling genetic engineers to transplant foreign genes into microorganisms to produce such valuable products as human insulin, which occurred in 1982.

Today, the field of biochemistry crosses over into many other sciences, as biochemists have become involved in genetics, biomedical engineering, biotechnology, nutrition, psychology, fertility, agriculture, and more. The new field of biotechnology is revolutionizing the pharmaceutical industry. Much of this work is done by biochemists and molecular biologists because this technology involves understanding the complex chemistry of life.

# THE JOB

Depending on their education level and area of specialty, biochemists can do many types of work for a variety of employers. For instance, a biochemist could do basic research for a federal government agency

## Biochemist Salaries

The following were the average annual salaries in 2009 for biochemists working in various industries:

| | |
|---|---|
| General medical and surgical hospitals | $105,840 |
| Scientific research and development services | $93,270 |
| Pharmaceutical and medicine manufacturing | $91,070 |
| Architectural and engineering services | $75,300 |
| Colleges and universities | $57,540 |

Source: U.S. Department of Labor

or for individual states with laboratories that employ skilled persons to analyze food, drug, air, water, waste, or animal tissue samples. A biochemist might work for a drug company as part of a basic research team searching for the cause of diseases or conduct applied research to develop drugs to cure disease. A biochemist might work in a biotechnology company focusing on the environment, energy, human health care, agriculture, or animal health. There, he or she might do research or quality control, or work on manufacturing/production or information systems. Another possibility is for the biochemist to specialize in an additional area, such as law, business, or journalism, and use his or her biochemistry or molecular biology background for a career that combines science with regulatory affairs, management, writing, or teaching.

Ph.D. scientists who enter the highest levels of academic life combine teaching and research. In addition to teaching in university classrooms and laboratories, they also do basic research designed to increase biochemistry and molecular biology knowledge. As Ph.D. scientists, these professionals could also work for an industry or government laboratory doing basic research or research and development (R&D). The problems studied, research styles, and type of organization vary widely across different laboratories. The Ph.D. scientist may lead a research group or be part of a small team of Ph.D. researchers. Other Ph.D. scientists might opt for administrative positions. In government, for example, these scientists might lead programs concerned with the safety of new devices, food, drugs, or pesticides and other chemicals. Or they might influence which projects will get federal funding.

Generally, biochemists employed in the United States work in one of three major fields: medicine, nutrition, or agriculture. In medicine, biochemists mass-produce life-saving chemicals usually found only in minuscule amounts in the body. Some of these chemicals have helped diabetics and heart attack victims for years. Biochemists employed in the field of medicine might work to identify chemical changes in organs or cells that signal the development of such diseases as cancer, diabetes, or schizophrenia. Or they may look for chemical explanations for why certain people develop muscular dystrophy or become obese. While studying chemical makeup and changes in these situations, biochemists may work to discover a treatment or a prevention for a disease. For instance, biochemists discovering how certain diseases such as AIDS and cancer escape detection by the immune system are also devising ways to enhance immunity to fight these diseases. Biochemists are also finding out the chemical basis of fertility and how to improve the success of in vitro fertilization to help couples have children or to preserve endangered species.

Biochemists in the pharmaceutical industry design, develop, and evaluate drugs, antibiotics, diagnostic kits, and other medical devices. They may search out ways to produce antibiotics, hormones, enzymes, or other drug components, or they may do quality control on the way in which drugs and dosages are made and determined.

In the field of nutrition, biochemists examine the effects of food on the body. For example, they might study the relationship between diet and diabetes. Biochemists doing this study could look at the nutrition content of certain foods eaten by people with diabetes and study how these foods affect the functioning of the pancreas and other organs. Biochemists in the nutrition field also look at vitamin and mineral deficiencies and how they affect the human body. They examine these deficiencies in relation to body performance, and they may study anything from how the liver is affected by a lack of vitamin B to the effects of poor nutrition on the ability to learn.

Biochemists involved in agriculture undertake studies to discover more efficient methods of crop cultivation, storage, and pest control. For example, they might create genetically engineered crops that are more resistant to frost, drought, spoilage, disease, and pests. They might focus on helping to create fruit trees that produce more fruit by studying the biochemical composition of the plant and determining how to alter or select for this desirable trait. Biochemists may study the chemical composition of insects to determine better and more efficient methods of controlling the pest population and the damage they do to crops. Or they could work

A biochemist studies the crystallization of amino acids as part of an experiment. *(Paul Sakuma, AP Photo)*

on programming bacteria to clean up the environment by "eating" toxic chemicals.

About seven out of 10 biochemists are engaged in basic research, often for a university medical school or nonprofit organization, such as a foundation or research institute. The remaining 30 percent do applied research, using the discoveries of basic research to solve practical problems or develop products. For example, a biochemist working in basic research may make a discovery about how a living organism forms hormones. This discovery will lead to a scientist doing applied research, making hormones in the laboratory, and eventually to mass production. Discoveries made in DNA research have led to techniques for identifying criminals from a single strand of hair or a tiny blood stain left at the scene of a crime. The distinction between basic and applied research is one of degree, however; biochemists often engage in both types of work.

Biochemistry requires skillful use of a wide range of sophisticated analytical equipment and application of newly discovered techniques requiring special instruments or new chemical reagents. Sometimes, biochemists themselves must invent and test new instruments if existing methods and equipment do not meet their needs. Biochemists must also be patient, methodical, and careful in their laboratory procedures.

# REQUIREMENTS

Although they usually specialize in one of many areas in the field, biochemists should also be familiar with several scientific disciplines, including chemistry, physics, mathematics, and computer science. High school classes can provide the foundation for getting this knowledge, while four years of college expands it, and postgraduate work directs students to explore specific areas more deeply. The following describes possible strategies at each level and includes a community college option.

## High School

If you have an interest in biochemistry as a high school student, you should take at least one year each of biology, chemistry, physics, algebra, geometry, and trigonometry. Introductory calculus is also a good idea. Because scientists must clearly and accurately communicate their results verbally and in writing, English courses that emphasize writing skills are strongly recommended. Many colleges and universities also require several years of a foreign language, a useful skill today, as scientists frequently exchange information with researchers from other countries.

## Postsecondary Training

Some biochemistry programs have their own special requirements for admission, so you should do a little research and take any special courses you need for the college that interests you. Also, check the catalogs of colleges and universities to see if they offer a program in biochemistry or related sciences. Some schools award a bachelor's degree in biochemistry, and nearly all colleges and universities offer a major in biology or chemistry.

To best prepare yourself for a career in biochemistry or molecular biology, you should start by earning a bachelor's degree in either of these two areas. Even if your college does not offer a specific program in biochemistry or molecular biology, you can get comparable training by doing one of two things: (1) working toward a bachelor's degree in chemistry and taking courses in biology, molecular genetics, and biochemistry, including a biochemistry laboratory class, or (2) earning a bachelor's degree in biology, but taking more chemistry, mathematics, and physics courses than the biology major may require, and also choosing a biochemistry course that has lab work with it.

It really doesn't matter if you earn a bachelor of science or a bachelor of arts degree; some schools offer both. It is more important to choose your courses thoughtfully and to get advice in your freshman year from a faculty member who knows about the fields of biochemistry and molecular biology.

Many careers in biochemistry, especially those that involve teaching at a college or directing scientific research at a university, a government laboratory, or a commercial company, require at least a master's degree and preferably a doctorate or Ph.D. degree. Because biochemistry is so broad-based, you can enter their graduate programs from such diverse fields as physics, psychology, nutrition, microbiology, or engineering. Graduate schools prefer students with laboratory or research experience.

However you get there, a graduate education program is intense. A master's degree requires about a year of course work and often a research project as well. For a Ph.D. degree, full-time course work can last up to two years, followed by one or more special test exams. But the most important part of Ph.D. training is the requirement for all students to conduct an extensive research project leading to significant new scientific findings. Most students work under a faculty member's direction. This training is vital, as it will help you develop the skills to frame scientific questions and discover ways to answer them. It will also teach you important laboratory skills useful in tackling other biochemical and biophysical problems. Most students complete a Ph.D. program in four or five years.

## Certification or Licensing

Biochemists who wish to work in a hospital may need certification by a national certifying board such as the American Board of Clinical Chemistry.

## Other Requirements

A scientist never stops learning, even when formal education has ended. This is particularly true for biochemists because constant breakthroughs and technology advances make for a constantly changing work environment. That is why most Ph.D.'s go for more research experience (postdoctoral research) before they enter the workplace. As a "postdoc," you would not take course work, earn a degree, or teach; you would likely work full time on a high-level research project in the laboratory of an established scientist. Typically, this postdoctoral period lasts two to three years, during which time you would get a salary or be supported by a fellowship. Though not essential for many industry research jobs, postdoctoral research is generally expected of those wishing to become professors. Also, because biochemistry and medicine are such allies, some Ph.D.

recipients also earn their medical degrees, or M.D.s, as a physician does. This is to get the broadest possible base for a career in medical research.

## EXPLORING

The analytical, specialized nature of biochemistry makes it unlikely that you will gain much exposure to it before college. Many high school chemistry, and biology courses, however, allow students to work with laboratory tools and techniques that will give them a valuable background before college. In some cases, high school students can take advantage of opportunities to train as laboratory technicians by taking courses at a community college. You might also want to contact local colleges, universities, or laboratories to set up interviews with biochemists to learn as much as you can about the field. In addition, reading science and medical magazines will help you to stay current with recent breakthroughs in the biochemistry field.

## EMPLOYERS

There are approximately 23,200 biochemists and biophysicists employed in the United States. Government agencies at the federal, state, and local levels employ four out of every 10 biological scientists. Some major governmental employers of biochemists include the National Institutes of Health, the Departments of Agriculture and Defense, the National Aeronautics and Space Administration, and national laboratories. At such agencies these scientists may do basic research and analyze food, drug, air, water, waste, or animal tissue samples. Biochemists also work for university medical schools or nonprofit organizations, such as a foundation or research institute, doing basic research. Drug companies employ biochemists to search for the causes of diseases or develop drugs to cure them. Biochemists work in quality control, research, manufacturing/production, or information systems at biotechnology companies that concentrate on the environment, energy, human health care, agriculture, or animal health. Universities hire biochemists to teach in combination with doing research.

## STARTING OUT

A bachelor's degree in biochemistry or molecular biology can help you get into medical, dental, veterinary, law, or business school. It can also be a stepping-stone to a career in many different but related fields: biotechnology, toxicology, biomedical engineering, clinical chemistry, plant pathology, animal science, or other fields. Biochemists fresh from a college undergraduate program can take advantage of opportunities to get valuable on-the-job experience in a biochemistry laboratory. The National Science Foundation and the National Institutes of Health, both federal government agencies, sponsor research programs for undergraduates. Groups who can particularly benefit from these programs include women, Hispanic Americans, African Americans, Native Americans, Native Alaskans, and students with disabilities. Your college or university may also offer senior research projects that provide hands-on experience.

Another way to improve your chances of getting a job is to spend an additional year at a university with training programs for specialized laboratory techniques. Researchers and companies like these "certificate programs" because they teach valuable skills related to cell culture, genetic engineering, recombinant DNA technology, biotechnology, in vitro cell biology, protein engineering, or DNA sequencing and synthesis. In some universities, you can work toward a bachelor's degree and a certificate at the same time.

Biochemists with bachelor's degrees usually begin work in industry or government as research assistants doing testing and analysis. In the drug industry, for example, you might analyze the ingredients of a product to verify and maintain its quality. Biochemists with master's degrees may enter the field in management, marketing, or sales positions, whereas those with doctorates usually go into basic or applied research. Many Ph.D. graduates work at colleges and universities where the emphasis is on teaching.

## ADVANCEMENT

The more education you have, the greater your reward potential. Biochemists with a graduate degree have more opportunities for advancement than those with only an undergraduate degree. It is not uncommon for students to go back to graduate school after working for a while in a job that required a lesser degree. Some graduate students become research or teaching assistants in colleges and universities, qualifying for professorships when they receive their advanced degrees. Having a doctorate allows you to design research initiatives and direct others in carrying out experiments. Experienced biochemists with doctorates can move up to high-level administrative positions and supervise entire research programs. Other highly qualified biochemists who prefer to devote themselves to research often become leaders in a particular aspect of their profession.

## EARNINGS

According to a report by the National Association of Colleges and Employers, beginning salaries in July 2009 for graduates with bachelor's degrees in biological and life sciences averaged $33,254 per year.

The U.S. Department of Labor (DOL) reports that biochemists and biophysicists had average annual incomes of $82,390 in 2009. Salaries ranged from less than $44,990 to more than $138,820 per year.

Colleges and universities also employ many biochemists as professors and researchers. The DOL reports that in 2009 the median salary for postsecondary chemistry teachers was $68,760, and biological science teachers made $73,980.

Biochemists who work for universities, the government, or industry all tend to receive good benefits packages, such as health and life insurance, pension plans, and paid vacation and sick leave. Those employed as university faculty operate on the academic calendar, which means that they can get summer and winter breaks from teaching classes.

## WORK ENVIRONMENT

Biochemists generally work in clean, quiet, and well-lighted laboratories where physical labor is minimal. They must, however, take the proper precautions in handling chemicals and organic substances that could be dangerous or cause illness. They may work with plants and animals; their tissues, cells, and products; and with yeast and bacteria.

Biochemists in industry generally work a 40-hour week, although they, like their counterparts in research, often put in many extra hours. They must be ready to spend a considerable amount of time keeping up with current literature, for example. Many biochemists occasionally travel to attend meetings or conferences. Those in research write papers for presentation at meetings or for publication in scientific journals.

Individuals interested in biochemistry must have the patience to work for long periods of time on a project without necessarily getting the desired results. Biochemistry is often a team affair, requiring an ability to work well and cooperate with others. Successful biochemists are continually learning and increasing their skills.

## OUTLOOK

Employment for biochemists is expected to grow much faster than the average for all occupations through 2018, according to the DOL.

Biotechnological research and development is fueling job growth. Employment is available in health-related fields, where the emphasis is on finding cures for such diseases as cancer, muscular dystrophy, HIV/AIDS, and Alzheimer's, and in other settings such as agricultural research. Additional jobs will be created to produce genetically engineered drugs and other products in the new and rapidly expanding field of genetic engineering. In this area, the outlook is best for biochemists with advanced degrees who can conduct genetic and cellular research. A caveat exists, however. Competition will be strong for basic research positions, and candidates with more education and the experience it brings will be more likely to find the positions they want. Additionally, employment growth may slow somewhat as the number of new biotechnology firms slows and existing firms merge. Biochemists with bachelor's degrees who have difficulty entering their chosen career field may find openings as technicians or technologists or may choose to transfer their skills to other biological science fields.

## FOR MORE INFORMATION

*For information about clinical laboratory careers, contact*
**American Association for Clinical Chemistry**
1850 K Street, NW, Suite 625
Washington, DC 20006-2215
Tel: 800-892-1400
http://www.aacc.org

*For general information about chemistry careers and approved education programs, contact*
**American Chemical Society**
1155 16th Street, NW
Washington, DC 20036-4839
Tel: 800-227-5558
E-mail: help@acs.org
http://www.chemistry.org

*For information on careers in the biological sciences, contact*
**American Institute of Biological Sciences**
1444 I Street, NW, Suite 200
Washington, DC 20005-6535
Tel: 202-628-1500
http://www.aibs.org

*For information on educational programs, contact*
**American Society for Biochemistry and Molecular Biology**
9650 Rockville Pike
Bethesda, MD 20814-3996
Tel: 301-634-7145
http://www.asbmb.org

*For career resources, contact*
**American Society for Investigative Pathology**
9650 Rockville Pike, Suite E133
Bethesda, MD 20814-3999
Tel: 301-634-7130
E-mail: asip@asip.org
http://www.asip.org

*For career information, including articles and books, contact*
**Biotechnology Industry Organization**
1201 Maryland Avenue, SW, Suite 900
Washington, DC 20024-2149
Tel: 202-962-9200
E-mail: info@bio.org
http://www.bio.org

# Biologists

## OVERVIEW

*Biologists* study the origin, development, anatomy, function, distribution, and other basic principles of living organisms. They are concerned with the nature of life itself in humans, microorganisms, plants, and animals, and with the relationship of each organism to its environment. Biologists perform research in many specialties that advance the fields of medicine, agriculture, and industry. Approximately 91,300 biological scientists are employed in the United States.

## HISTORY

The biological sciences developed slowly over the course of human history. Early humans practiced an inexact form of biology when they established agriculture. They observed the environment around them to determine what types of seeds yielded consumable food, when to plant, when to water, and when to harvest the seeds for planting in the next season. Early humans improved their way of life as a result of their primitive forays into science.

It wasn't until modern times that biology developed into an exact science. Our ancestors learned to differentiate between desirable and undesirable plants (taxonomy), to seek out and live in more habitable environments (ecology), to domesticate plants (agronomy and horticulture) and animals (animal husbandry), and to eat a suitable diet (nutrition). Eventually, plants and animals were classified; later they were studied to see how they functioned and how they related to other organisms

### QUICK FACTS

**School Subjects**
Biology
Earth science
Physiology

**Personal Skills**
Mechanical/manipulative
Technical/scientific

**Work Environment**
Indoors and outdoors
Primarily multiple locations

**Minimum Education Level**
Bachelor's degree

**Salary Range**
$33,254 to $66,510 to $100,580+

**Certification or Licensing**
Voluntary (certification)
Required for certain positions (licensing)

**Outlook**
Much faster than the average

**DOT**
041

**GOE**
02.03.03

**NOC**
2121

**O*NET-SOC**
19-1020.01, 19-1029.00

around them. This was the beginning of zoology (animal science) and botany (plant science).

The Greek philosopher Aristotle created one of the first documented taxonomic systems for animals. He divided animals into two types: blooded (mammals, birds, amphibians, reptiles, and fishes) and bloodless (insects, crustaceans, and other lower animals). He also studied reproduction and theorized, incorrectly, how embryos developed in animals.

From the second century to the 11th century, the Arabs made important advances in biological understanding. Unlike the Europeans, they continued to study from the base of knowledge established by the Greeks. Avicenna, a Persian philosopher and physician, wrote the *Canon of Medicine*, one of the most influential and important publications on medical knowledge in the world at its time—and for the next seven centuries.

The field of biology has expanded rapidly in the last two centuries. The French physician Louis Pasteur developed the field of immunology, and his studies of fermentation led to modern microbiology. Many other achievements became possible because of improvements in the microscope. Scientists could isolate much smaller structures than ever before possible. Matthias Schleiden and Theodor Schwann formulated the idea that the cell is the fundamental unit of all organisms. Gregor Mendel discovered the principles of heredity through the study of peas.

While the 19th century can be considered the age of cellular biology, the 20th and early 21st centuries have been dominated by studies and breakthroughs in biochemistry and molecular biology. The discovery of the atomic structure allowed the fundamental building blocks of nature to be studied. Living tissues were found to be composed of fats, sugars, and proteins. Proteins were found to be composed of amino acids. Discoveries in cell biology established the manner in which information was transmitted from one organism to its progeny. Chromosomes were recognized as the carriers of this information. In 1944, Oswald Avery and a team of scientists were able to isolate and identify DNA as the transmitter of genetic information. In 1953 James Watson and Francis Crick deciphered the complex structure of DNA and predicted that it carried the genetic code for all living matter.

Today, advances in biotechnology have allowed biologists and other scientists to study and manipulate the DNA of plants and animals to create healthier organisms and more productive yields, as well as seek out cures to human diseases. In addition to medicine, scientists are using biotechnology in agriculture and environmental remediation.

Biological science is the foundation for most of the discoveries that affect people's everyday lives. Biologists break new ground to improve our health and quality of life and help us to better understand the world around us.

## THE JOB

Biology can be divided into many specialties. The biologist, who studies a wide variety of living organisms, has interests that differ from those of the chemist, physicist, and geologist, who are concerned with nonliving matter. Biologists, or life scientists, may be identified by their specialties. Following is a breakdown of the many kinds of biologists and their specific fields of study.

*Anatomists* study animal bodies from basic cell structure to complex tissues and organs. They determine the ability of body parts to regenerate and investigate the possibility of transplanting organs and skin. Their research is applied to human medicine.

*Aquatic biologists* study animals and plants that live in water and how they are affected by their environmental conditions, such as the salt, acid, and oxygen content of the water and temperature, light, and other factors.

*Biochemists* study the chemical composition of living organisms. They attempt to understand the complex reactions involved in reproduction, growth, metabolism, and heredity. (For more information, see the article Biochemists.)

*Biophysicists* apply physical principles to biological problems. They study the mechanics, heat, light, radiation, sound, electricity, and energetics of living cells and organisms and do research in the areas of vision, hearing, brain function, nerve conduction, muscle reflex, and damaged cells and tissues.

*Biotechnicians*, or *biological technicians*, assist the cornucopia of biological scientists in their endeavors.

*Botanists* study plant life. Some specialize in plant biochemistry, the structure and function of plant parts, and identification and classification, among other topics. (For more information, see the article Botanists.)

*Cytologists*, sometimes called *cell biologists*, examine the cells of plants and animals, including those cells involved in reproduction. They use microscopes and other instruments to observe the growth and division of cells and to study the influences of physical and chemical factors on both normal and malignant cells.

*Ecologists* examine such factors as pollutants, rainfall, altitude, temperature, and population size in order to study the distribution and abundance of organisms and their relation to their environment.

*Entomologists* study insects and their relationship to other life forms.

*Geneticists*, also known as *genetic scientists*, study heredity in various forms of life. They are concerned with how biological traits such as color, size, and resistance to disease originate and are transmitted from one generation to another. They also try to develop ways to alter or produce new traits, using chemicals, heat, light, or other means. (For more information, see the article Genetic Scientists.)

*Histopathologists* investigate diseased tissue in humans and animals.

*Immunologists* study the manner in which the human body resists disease.

*Limnologists* study freshwater organisms and their environment.

*Marine biologists* specialize in the study of marine species and their environment. They gather specimens at different times, taking into account tidal cycles, seasons, and exposure to atmospheric elements, in order to answer questions concerning the overall health of sea organisms and their environment. (For more information, see the article Marine Biologists.)

*Microbiologists* study bacteria, viruses, molds, algae, yeasts, and other organisms of microscopic or submicroscopic size. Some microorganisms are useful to humans; they are studied and used in the production of food, such as cheese, bread, and tofu. Other microorganisms have been used to preserve food and tenderize meat. Some microbiologists work with microorganisms that cause disease. They work to diagnose, treat, and prevent disease. Microbiologists have helped prevent typhoid fever, influenza, measles, polio, whooping cough, and smallpox. Today, they work on cures for AIDS, cancer, cystic fibrosis, and Alzheimer's disease, among others. (For more information, see the article Microbiologists.)

*Molecular biologists* apply their research on animal and bacterial systems toward the goal of improving and better understanding human health.

*Mycologists* study edible, poisonous, and parasitic fungi, such as mushrooms, molds, yeasts, and mildews, to determine which are useful to medicine, agriculture, and industry. Their research has resulted in benefits such as the development of antibiotics, the propagation of mushrooms, and methods of retarding fabric deterioration.

*Nematologists* study nematodes (roundworms), which are parasitic in animals and plants. Nematodes transmit diseases, attack insects, or attack other nematodes that exist in soil or water. Nematologists investigate and develop methods of controlling these organisms.

*Parasitologists* study animal parasites and their effects on humans and other animals.

*Pharmacologists* may be employed as researchers by pharmaceutical companies. They often spend most of their time working in the laboratory, where they study the effects of various drugs and medical compounds on mice or rabbits. Working within controlled environments, pharmacologists precisely note the types, quantities, and timing of medicines administered as a part of their experiments. Periodically, they make blood smears or perform autopsies to study different reactions. They usually work with a team of researchers, headed by one with a doctorate and consisting of several biologists with master's and bachelor's degrees and some laboratory technicians.

*Physiologists* are biologists who specialize in studying all the life stages of plants or animals. Some specialize in a particular body system or a particular function, such as respiration.

*Wildlife biologists* study the habitats and the conditions necessary for the survival of birds and other wildlife. Their goal is to find ways to ensure the continuation of healthy wildlife populations, while lessening the impact and growth of civilization around them.

*Zoologists* study all types of animals to learn their origin, interrelationships, classifications, life histories, habits, diseases, relation to the environment, growth, genetics, and distribution. Zoologists are usually identified by the animals they study: *ichthyologists* (fish), *mammalogists* (mammals), *ornithologists* (birds), and *herpetologists* (reptiles and amphibians). (For more information, see the article Zoologists.)

Biologists may also work for government agencies concerned with public health. *Toxicologists*, for example, study the effects of toxic substances on humans, animals, and plants. The data they gather are used in consumer protection and industrial safety programs to reduce the hazards of accidental exposure or ingestion. (For more information, see the article Toxicologists.) *Public-health microbiologists* conduct experiments on water, foods, and the general environment of a community to detect the presence of harmful bacteria so pollution and contagious diseases can be controlled or eliminated.

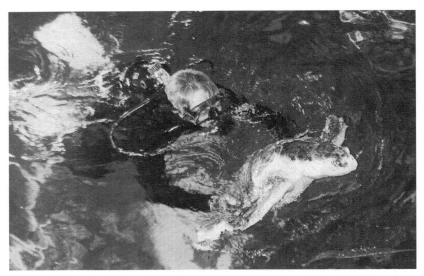

A biologist at the New England Aquarium accompanies a young Kemp's Ridley sea turtle through the main tank's water en route to its annual physical exam. *(Stephan Savoia, AP Photo)*

## REQUIREMENTS

### High School

High school students interested in a career in biology should take English, biology, physics, chemistry, Latin, geometry, and algebra.

### Postsecondary Training

Prospective biologists should also obtain a broad undergraduate college training. In addition to courses in all phases of biology, useful related courses include organic and inorganic chemistry, physics, and mathematics. Modern languages, English, biometrics (the use of mathematics in biological measurements), and statistics are also useful. Courses in computers will be extremely beneficial. Students should take advantage of courses that require laboratory, field, or collecting work.

Nearly all institutions offer undergraduate training in one or more of the biological sciences. These vary from liberal arts schools that offer basic majors in botany and zoology to large universities that permit specialization in areas such as entomology, bacteriology, and physiology at the undergraduate level.

The best way to become a biologist is to earn a bachelor's degree in biology or one of its specialized fields, such as anatomy, bacteriology, botany, ecology, or microbiology. For the highest professional status, a doctorate is required. This is particularly true of top research positions and most higher-level college teaching openings. Many colleges and universities offer courses leading to a master's degree and a doctorate.

Candidates for a doctorate specialize in one of the subdivisions of biology. A number of sources of financial assistance are available to finance graduate work. Most major universities have a highly developed fellowship (scholarship) or assistantship (part-time teaching or research) program.

Organizations, such as the U.S. Public Health Service and the National Science Foundation, make awards to support graduate students. In addition, major universities often hold research contracts or have their own projects that provide part-time and summer employment for undergraduate and graduate students.

## Certification or Licensing

Several professional associations, such as the Ecological Society of America and the American Society for Microbiology, offer voluntary professional certification to biologists who specialize in a particular field.

A state license may be required for biologists who are employed as technicians in general service health organizations, such as hospitals or clinics. To qualify for this license, proof of suitable educational background is necessary.

## Other Requirements

Biologists must be systematic in their approach to solving the problems that they face. They should have probing, inquisitive minds and an aptitude for biology, chemistry, and mathematics. Patience and imagination are also required since they may spend much time in observation and analysis. Biologists must also have good communication skills in order to effectively gather and exchange data and solve problems that arise in their work.

# EXPLORING

You can measure your aptitude and interest in the work of the biologist by taking courses in the field. Laboratory assignments, for example, provide information on techniques used by the working biologist. Many schools hire students as laboratory assistants to work directly under a teacher and help administer the laboratory sections of courses.

School assemblies, field trips to federal and private laboratories and research centers, and career conferences provide additional insight into career opportunities. Advanced students often are able to attend professional meetings and seminars.

Part-time and summer positions in biology or related areas are particularly helpful. Students with some college courses in biology may find summer positions as laboratory assistants. Graduate students may find work on research projects conducted by their institutions. Beginning college and advanced high school students may find employment as laboratory aides or hospital orderlies or attendants. Despite the menial nature of these positions, they afford a useful insight into careers in biology. High school students often have the opportunity to join volunteer service groups at local hospitals. Student science training programs allow qualified high school students to spend a summer doing research under the supervision of a scientist.

## EMPLOYERS

There are approximately 91,300 biologists employed in the United States. About 40 percent of all biological scientists work for the government at the federal, state, or local level. The majority of those who do not work for the government are involved in the drug industry, which includes pharmaceutical companies, hospitals, biotechnology companies, and laboratories. The area in which biologists work is influenced by their specialties. Marine biologists, for example, can find employment with the U.S. Department of Interior, the U.S. Fish and Wildlife Service, and the National Oceanic and Atmospheric Administration. They may also find employment in nongovernmental agencies, such as the Scripps Institution of Oceanography in California and the Marine Biological Laboratory in Massachusetts. Microbiologists can find employment with the U.S. Department of Health and Human Services, the Environmental Protection Agency, and the Department of Agriculture, among others. They may also work for pharmaceutical, food, agricultural, geological, environmental, and pollution control companies. Wildlife biologists can find employment in the U.S. Public Health Service, the U.S. Fish and Wildlife Service, the National Park Service, and the Forest Service, among many others.

## STARTING OUT

Biologists who are interested in becoming teachers should consult their college career services offices. Public and private high schools and an increasing number of colleges hire teachers through the colleges at which they studied. Private employment agencies also place a significant number of teachers. Some teaching positions are filled through direct application.

Biologists interested in private industry and nonprofit organizations may also apply directly for employment. Major organizations that employ biologists often interview college seniors on campus. Private and public employment offices frequently have listings from these employers. Experienced biologists often change positions as a result of contacts made at professional seminars and national conventions.

Special application procedures are required for positions with government agencies. Civil service applications for federal, state, and municipal positions may be obtained by writing to the agency involved and from high school and college guidance and career services offices, public employment agencies, and post offices.

## ADVANCEMENT

In a field as broad as biology, numerous opportunities for advancement exist. To a great extent, however, advancement depends on the individual's level of education. A doctorate is generally required for college teaching, independent research, and top-level administrative and management jobs. A master's degree is sufficient for some jobs in applied research, and a bachelor's degree may qualify for some entry-level jobs.

With the right qualifications, the biologist may advance to the position of project chief and direct a team of other biologists. Many use their knowledge and experience as background for administrative and management positions. Often, as they develop professional expertise, biologists move from strictly technical assignments into positions in which they interpret biological knowledge.

The usual path of advancement in biology, as in other sciences, comes from specialization and the development of the status of an expert in a given field. Biologists may work with professionals in other major fields to explore problems that require an interdisciplinary approach, such as biochemistry, biophysics, and biostatistics (or biometrics). Biochemistry, for example, uses the methods of chemistry to study the composition of biological materials and the molecular mechanisms of biological processes.

## EARNINGS

Earnings for biological scientists vary extensively based on the type and size of their employer, the individual's level of education and experience, and the area of biology in which the scientist specializes. The U.S. Department of Labor (DOL) reports that biologists earned the following mean annual salaries in 2009 by specialty: biochemistry and biophysics, $88,550; microbiology, $71,980; soil and plant science, $65,180; and zoology and wildlife biology, $60,670. The DOL reports that the median salary for biological scientists, not otherwise classified was $66,510 in 2009. Salaries ranged from less than $36,750 to $100,580 or more.

According to the National Association of Colleges and Employers, those with bachelor's degrees in the biological and life sciences received average starting salaries of $33,254 in July 2009.

In general, the highest salaries were earned by biologists in business and industry, followed by those self-employed, working for nonprofit organizations, in military service, and working for the U.S. Public Health Service or other positions in the federal government. The lowest salaries were earned by teachers and by those working for various state and local governments.

Biologists are usually eligible for health and dental insurance, paid vacations and sick days, and retirement plans. Some employers may offer reimbursement for continuing education, seminars, and travel.

## WORK ENVIRONMENT

The biologist's work environment varies greatly depending upon the position and type of employer. One biologist may work outdoors or travel much of the time. Another wears a white smock and spends years working in a laboratory. Some work with toxic substances and disease cultures; strict safety measures must be observed.

Biologists frequently work under pressure. For example, those employed by pharmaceutical houses work in an atmosphere of keen competition for sales that encourages the development of new drug products, and, as they are identified, the rapid testing and early marketing of these products. The work is very exacting, however, and pharmaceutical biologists must exercise great care to ensure that adequate testing of products has been properly conducted.

Some biologists, including botanists, ecologists, and zoologists, may undertake strenuous, sometimes dangerous, fieldwork in primitive conditions. Marine biologists work in the field, on research ships or in laboratories, in tropical seas and ocean areas with considerably cooler climates. They will be required to perform some strenuous work, such as carrying a net, digging, chipping, or hauling equipment or specimens. Marine biologists who work underwater must be able to avoid hazards, such as razor-sharp coral reefs and other underwater dangers. Wildlife biologists work in all types of weather and in all types of terrain and ecosystems. They may work alone or with a group in inhospitable surroundings in order to gather information.

## OUTLOOK

The DOL predicts that employment for biological scientists will grow much faster than the average for all careers through 2018. Companies developing new drugs, modified crops, environmentally friendly products, and the like will need the expertise of biological scientists. The DOL also predicts that even companies not solely involved in biotechnology will be increasingly using biotechnology developments and techniques in their businesses. This should cause more job opportunities for biological scientists in a variety of industries. Private industry will need biologists to work in sales, marketing, and research management.

There will also be strong demand for biologists to study, clean up, and protect the environment. They will be in demand by environmental regulatory agencies and lawmakers who need expertise regarding the environment. There will be fewer opportunities in botany and zoology because these fields are so small, and there is less job turnover. Employment in marine biology is predicted to be especially competitive.

Biologists with advanced degrees will be best qualified for the most lucrative and challenging jobs, although this varies by specialty, with genetic, cellular, and biochemical research showing the most promise. Competition will be stiff for basic research positions. Scientists with bachelor's degrees may find openings as science or engineering technicians, health technologists and technicians, and high school biology teachers. Many colleges and universities are cutting back on their faculties, but high schools and two-year colleges may have teaching positions available.

## FOR MORE INFORMATION

*For information on careers in biology, contact*
   **American Institute of Biological Sciences**
   1444 I Street, NW, Suite 200
   Washington, DC 20005-6535
   Tel: 202-628-1500
   http://www.aibs.org

*For a career brochure, career-related articles, and a list of institutions that award academic degrees with a major in physiology, contact*
**American Physiological Society**
9650 Rockville Pike
Bethesda, MD 20814-3991
Tel: 301-634-7164
http://www.the-aps.org

*For information on educational programs, contact*
**American Society for Biochemistry and Molecular Biology**
9650 Rockville Pike
Bethesda, MD 20814-3996
Tel: 301-634-7145
http://www.asbmb.org

*For information on careers, educational resources, and fellowships, contact*
**American Society for Microbiology**
1752 N Street, NW
Washington, DC 20036-2904
Tel: 202-737-3600
http://www.asm.org

*For general information about plant biology, contact*
**American Society of Plant Biologists**
http://my.aspb.org

*For career information, including articles and books about the biotechnology industry, contact*
**Biotechnology Industry Organization**
1201 Maryland Avenue, SW, Suite 900
Washington, DC 20024-2149
Tel: 202-962-9200
E-mail: info@bio.org
http://www.bio.org

*For information on botany careers, contact*
**Botanical Society of America**
PO Box 299
St. Louis, MO 63166-0299
Tel: 314-577-9566
E-mail: bsa-manager@botany.org
http://www.botany.org

*In addition to certification, the ESA offers a wide variety of publications, including* Issues in Ecology, Careers in Ecology, *and fact sheets about specific ecological concerns. For more information, contact*

**Ecological Society of America (ESA)**
1990 M Street, NW, Suite 700
Washington, DC 20036-3415
Tel: 202-833-8773
E-mail: esahq@esa.org
http://www.esa.org

*For information on specific careers in biology, contact*
**National Institutes of Health**
9000 Rockville Pike
Bethesda, MD 20892-0001
Tel: 301-496-4000
E-mail: NIHinfo@od.nih.gov
http://www.nih.gov

*For information on specific careers, visit the administration's Web site.*
**U.S. Food and Drug Administration**
10903 New Hampshire Avenue
Silver Spring, MD 20993-0002
Tel: 888-463-6332
http://www.fda.gov

# Biomedical Engineers

## QUICK FACTS

**School Subjects**
Biology
Chemistry

**Personal Skills**
Helping/teaching
Technical/scientific

**Work Environment**
Primarily indoors
Primarily one location

**Minimum Education Level**
Bachelor's degree

**Salary Range**
$49,480 to $78,860 to
$123,270+

**Certification or Licensing**
Required for certain positions

**Outlook**
Much faster than the average

**DOT**
019

**GOE**
02.07.04

**NOC**
2148

**O*NET-SOC**
17-2031.00

## OVERVIEW

*Biomedical engineers* are highly trained scientists who use engineering and life science principles to research biological aspects of animal and human life. They develop new theories, and they modify, test, and prove existing theories on life systems. They design health care instruments and devices or apply engineering principles to the study of human systems. There are approximately 16,000 biomedical engineers employed in the United States.

## HISTORY

Biomedical engineering is one of many new professions created by advancements in technology. It is an interdisciplinary field that brings together two respected professions: biology and engineering.

Biology is the study of life, and engineering, in broad terms, studies sources of energy in nature and the properties of matter in a way that is useful to humans, particularly in machines, products, and structures. A combination of the two fields, biomedical engineering developed primarily after 1945, as new technology allowed for the application of engineering principles to biology. The artificial heart is just one in a long list of the products of biomedical engineering. Other products include artificial organs, prosthetics, the use of lasers in surgery, cryosurgery, and ultrasonics, and the use of computers and thermography in diagnosis.

## THE JOB

Using engineering principles to solve medical- and health-related problems, the biomedical engineer works closely with life scientists,

## Biomedical Engineer Salaries

The following were the average annual salaries in 2009 for biomedical engineers working in various industries:

| | |
|---|---|
| Navigational, measuring, electromedical, and control instruments manufacturing | $92,330 |
| Scientific research and development services | $86,150 |
| Medical equipment and supplies manufacturing | $81,590 |
| Pharmaceutical and medicine manufacturing | $81,150 |
| General medical and surgical hospitals | $66,250 |

Source: U.S. Department of Labor

members of the medical profession, and chemists. Most of the work revolves around the laboratory. There are three interrelated work areas: research, design, and teaching.

Biomedical research is multifaceted and broad in scope. It calls upon engineers to apply their knowledge of mechanical, chemical, and electrical engineering as well as anatomy and physiology in the study of living systems. Using computers, biomedical engineers use their knowledge of graphic and related technologies to develop mathematical models that simulate physiological systems.

In biomedical engineering design, medical instruments and devices are developed. Engineers work on artificial organs, ultrasonic imagery devices, cardiac pacemakers, and surgical lasers, for example. They design and build systems that will update hospital, laboratory, and clinical procedures. They also train health care personnel in the proper use of this new equipment.

Biomedical engineering is taught on the university level. Teachers conduct classes, advise students, serve on academic committees, and supervise or conduct research.

Within biomedical engineering, an individual may concentrate on a particular specialty area. Some of the well-established specialties are *biomechanics, biomaterials, bioinstrumentation, systems physiology, orthopedic engineering*, and *rehabilitation engineering*. These specialty areas frequently depend on one another.

Biomechanics is mechanics applied to biological or medical problems. Examples include the artificial heart, the artificial kidney, and the artificial hip. Biomaterials is the study of the optimal materials with which to construct such devices, bioinstrumentation is the science of measuring physiological functions. Systems physiology uses engineering strategies, techniques, and tools to gain a comprehensive and integrated understanding of living organisms ranging from bacteria to humans. Biomedical engineers in this specialty examine such things as the biochemistry of metabolism and the control of limb movements. Orthopedic engineering is the application of biomedical engineering to diseases and conditions of the musculoskeletal system. Rehabilitation engineering is a new and growing specialty area of biomedical engineering. Its goal is to expand the capabilities and improve the quality of life for individuals with physical impairments. Rehabilitation engineers often work directly with the disabled person and modify equipment for individual use.

## REQUIREMENTS

### High School

You can best prepare for a career as a biomedical engineer by taking courses in biology, chemistry, physics, mathematics, drafting, and computers. Communication and problem-solving skills are necessary, so classes in English, writing, and logic are important. Participating in science clubs and competing in science fairs will give you the opportunity to design and invent systems and products.

### Postsecondary Training

Most biomedical engineers have an undergraduate degree in biomedical engineering or a related field and a Ph.D. in some facet of biomedical engineering. Undergraduate study is roughly divided into halves. The first two years are devoted to theoretical subjects, such as abstract physics and differential equations in addition to the core curriculum most undergraduates take. The third and fourth years include more applied science. Worldwide, there are more than 100 colleges and universities that offer programs in biomedical engineering. In the United States, biomedical engineering programs are accredited by the Accreditation Board for Engineering and Technology (http://www.abet.org).

During graduate programs, students work on research or product development projects headed by faculty.

### Certification or Licensing

Engineers whose work may affect the life, health, or safety of the public must be registered according to regulations in all 50 states and the District of Columbia. Applicants for registration must have received a degree from an American Board for Engineering and Technology-accredited engineering program and have four years of experience. They must also pass a written examination administered by the state in which they wish to work.

### Other Requirements
You should have a strong commitment to learning if you plan on becoming a biomedical engineer. You should be scientifically inclined and be able to apply that knowledge in problem solving. Becoming a biomedical engineer requires long years of schooling because a biomedical engineer needs to be an expert in the fields of engineering and biology. Also, biomedical engineers have to be familiar with chemical, material, and electrical engineering as well as physiology and computers.

## EXPLORING

Undergraduate courses offer a great deal of exposure to the field. Working in a hospital where biomedical engineers are employed can also provide you with insight into the field, as can interviews with practicing or retired biomedical engineers. You can also read Planning a Career in Biomedical Engineering, which can be found at the Biomedical Engineering Society's Web site, http://www.bmes.org.

## EMPLOYERS

There are approximately 16,000 biomedical engineers working in the United States. About 20 percent are employed in scientific research and development and 20 percent work in medical equipment and supplies manufacturing. In addition, many biomedical engineers are employed in hospitals and medical institutions, and in research and educational facilities. Employment opportunities also exist in government regulatory agencies.

## STARTING OUT

A variety of routes may be taken to gain employment as a biomedical engineer. Recent graduates may use college career services offices, or they may apply directly to employers, often to personnel offices in hospitals and industry. A job may be secured by answering an advertisement in the employment section of a newspaper. Information on job openings is also available at state employment offices and the federal Office of Personnel Management (http://usajobs.opm.gov). Additionally, the Biomedical Engineering Society offers job listings at its Web site, http://www.bmes.org.

## ADVANCEMENT

Advancement opportunities are tied directly to educational and research background. In a nonteaching capacity, a biomedical engineer with an advanced degree can rise to a supervisory position. In teaching, a doctorate is usually necessary to become a full professor. By demonstrating excellence in research, teaching, and departmental committee involvement, one can move from instructor to assistant professor and then to full professor, department chair, or even dean.

Qualifying for and receiving research grant funding can also be a means of advancing one's career in both the nonteaching and teaching sectors.

## EARNINGS

The amount a biomedical engineer earns is dependent upon education, experience, and type of employer. According to the U.S. Department of Labor, biomedical engineers had a median yearly income of $78,860 in 2009. At the low end of the pay scale, 10 percent earned less than $49,480 per year, and at the high end, 10 percent earned more than $123,270 annually.

According to a July 2009 survey by the National Association of Colleges and Employers, the average beginning salary for biomedical engineers with bachelor's degrees was $54,158.

Biomedical engineers can expect benefits from employers, including health insurance, paid vacation and sick days, and retirement plans.

## WORK ENVIRONMENT

Biomedical engineers who teach in a university will have much student contact in the classroom, the laboratory, and the office. They also will be expected to serve on relevant committees while continuing their teaching, research, and writing responsibilities. As competition for teaching positions increases, the requirement that professors publish papers will increase. Professors usually are responsible for obtaining government or private research grants to support their work.

Those who work in industry and government have much contact with other professionals, including chemists, medical scientists, and doctors. They often work as part of a team, testing and developing new products. All biomedical engineers who do lab work are in clean, well-lighted environments, using sophisticated equipment.

## OUTLOOK

There will be great need for skilled biomedical engineers in the future. Prospects look particularly good in the health care industry, which will continue to grow rapidly, primarily because people are living longer and require better medical devices and equipment. The U.S. Department of Labor predicts that employment for biomedical engineers will increase much faster than the average for all occupations through 2018. New jobs will become available in biomedical research in prosthetics, pharmaceutical manufacturing and related industries (especially in cost-management settings), the development of artificial internal organs, computer applications, and instrumentation and other medical systems. In addition, a demand will exist for professors to train the biomedical engineers needed to fill these positions.

Because of the increased demand for biomedical engineers, the number of degrees granted in the field has increased significantly. Graduates with a bachelor's degree will face stiff competition for entry-level jobs. Thus, people entering this field are strongly encouraged to pursue a graduate degree to increase their job prospects.

## FOR MORE INFORMATION

*For information on medical and biological engineering, contact*
American Institute for Medical and Biological Engineering
1701 K Street, NW, Suite 510
Washington, DC 20036-1520
Tel: 202-496-9660
http://www.aimbe.org

*For more information on careers in biomedical engineering, contact*
American Society for Engineering Education
1818 N Street, NW, Suite 600
Washington, DC 20036-2479
Tel: 202-331-3500
http://www.asee.org

*For information on careers, student chapters, and to read* Planning
a Career in Biomedical Engineering, *contact or visit the following
Web site:*
   **Biomedical Engineering Society**
   8401 Corporate Drive, Suite 1125
   Landover, MD 20785-2224
   Tel: 301-459-1999
   E-mail: info@bmes.org
   http://www.bmes.org

*For career information, including articles and books on the biotech-
nology industry, contact*
   **Biotechnology Industry Organization**
   1201 Maryland Avenue, SW, Suite 900
   Washington, DC 20024-2149
   Tel: 202-962-9200
   E-mail: info@bio.org
   http://www.bio.org

*For information on high school programs that provide opportuni-
ties to learn about engineering technology, contact JETS.*
   **Junior Engineering Technical Society (JETS)**
   1420 King Street, Suite 405
   Alexandria, VA 22314-2750
   Tel: 703-548-5387
   E-mail: info@jets.org
   http://www.jets.org

*For Canadian career information, contact*
   **Canadian Medical and Biological Engineering Society**
   1485 Laperriere Avenue
   Ottawa, ON K1Z 7S8 Canada
   http://www.cmbes.ca

*Visit the following Web site for more information on educational
programs, job listings, grants, and links to other biomedical engineering sites:*
   **BMETnet: The Biomedical Engineering Network**
   http://www.bmenet.org

# Biotechnology Patent Lawyers

## OVERVIEW

*Biotechnology patent lawyers* are lawyers who specialize in helping biotechnology researchers, scientists, and research corporations with all legal aspects of their biotechnology patents. They assist clients in applying for patents and enforcing those patents. Although some of their duties may be similar to those of intellectual property lawyers, these lawyers focus on work involving the biotechnology field.

## HISTORY

Biotechnology patent law is a blending of two fields: science and law. The field of science dates back thousands of years. Ancient Egyptians, for example, organized knowledge about matter into systems, which was the beginning of chemistry. In the 4th century B.C., the field of biology advanced with the work of Greek philosopher Aristotle who created taxonomic (classification) systems for animals. The 11th-century Persian philosopher and physician Avicenna wrote the *Canon of Medicine*, a compendium of medical knowledge. In the 19th century, Louis Pasteur, Matthias Schleiden, and Theodor Schwann contributed to the growth of the field of microbiology; Gregor Mendel discovered the principles of genetics through his studies of peas. The modern history of genetics can be traced back to the early 1950s when James Watson and Francis Crick discovered the double helix structure of DNA, the genetic material that makes up the most basic component of living organisms. After that came the discovery of recombinant DNA techniques and finally the ability to genetically engineer cells and clone (make copies of) desired genes. These scientific advancements have resulted in such developments as nontoxic pesticides, longer-lasting vegetables, advanced blood tests, and even Dolly, the cloned Scottish sheep.

The history of law also dates back thousands of years, although the area of patent law has been a relatively recent development. Dating back to the 1700s, people sought help from lawyers to protect their ideas and inventions from theft. Unfortunately, both lawyers and their clients were often frustrated in their attempts to gain support for patents and copyrights in court. By the 20th century, however, Congress and courts had begun to see innovative ideas and products as valuable to U.S. status in the global market. Today, scientists, researchers, and research companies involved with biotechnology rely on patent law to ensure that their discoveries and advancements are protected as their property. Biotechnology patent lawyers are the unique bridge between the scientific and legal worlds, making sure their clients receive the acknowledgements for and profits from their scientific work.

## THE JOB

The biotechnology patent lawyer's job actually begins only after researchers or scientists have done extensive work in their field. For example, researchers or scientists may draw on advances in molecular and cellular biology, genetics, and knowledge of the human immune system, to change and combine DNA in an effort to come up with a new vaccine. When they have developed this vaccine, they are ready to seek a patent for their invention from the U.S. Patent and Trademark Office. At this point, biotechnology patent lawyers join the process to help these researchers and research corporations with all legal aspects of their biotechnology patents. A patent gives the patent holder the right to exclude others from making, using, or selling an invention for a specific period of time.

Biotechnology patent lawyers have extensive scientific and legal knowledge. Like any other lawyer, they must be able to give clients legal advice and represent them in court when necessary. In addition, their scientific knowledge helps them prepare patent specifications for their clients' work.

For most biotechnology patent attorneys, the job falls into three major categories. First, they take their clients' patent claims before the U.S. Patent and Trademark Office and attempt to obtain patents for them. Second, they negotiate various kinds of business transactions that involve patents. For example, they might assist a client in licensing the rights to use or sell a certain patented technology. Third, biotechnology lawyers assist clients in the enforcement of patents, which might involve suing another party for patent infringement or defending a client from an infringement lawsuit. While some patent attorneys may find that most of their cases fall into one or the other of these categories, most patent attorneys take on cases in all three of these areas.

According to Lawrence Foster, a biotechnology patent attorney who practices on the East Coast, the best part of biotech practice is the chance to learn about the latest scientific discoveries and developments. "You can open a newspaper and see the first article will feature something you've known about for months," he remarks. "It's exciting to know that you're learning about these discoveries as they happen, long before most people have any idea." Although lawyers must keep these often thrilling developments quiet to protect their clients' confidentiality, they still have the satisfaction of knowing that they're party to the latest inventions in genetic and even cloning technology.

## REQUIREMENTS

### High School

To prepare for this field, take college preparatory classes in high school that include both the sciences, such as biology and chemistry, and government or law. In addition, take mathematics and economics classes, which will give you practice working with numbers and theories. Take history or social studies courses, which will provide you with an understanding of the development of societies. Since much of your professional time will be spent researching documents, writing patent specifications, and presenting arguments, be sure to take English classes. These classes will help you develop your writing, speaking, and research skills. Finally, since many colleges have a foreign language requirement and biotechnology work takes place around the world, consider adding a language to your class schedule.

### Postsecondary Training

Because this is a specialized field, you will need several years of postsecondary training that include undergraduate and graduate level work. Like any lawyer, you will need to get a college degree before attending law school. A liberal arts background is the most common. In addition to such courses as English, government, and economics, you will also want to load up on science courses and should consider majoring in one of the sciences. In fact, biotechnology patent lawyers in the greatest demand typically have Ph.D.'s in a science field, such as genetic engineering, as well as their law degree. After college, a Ph.D. in one of the sciences may take between four and five years to complete. Law school typically lasts three years for full-time students. As part of their entrance requirements, most law schools require potential students to take the Law School Admission Test (LSAT), which measures critical thinking and reasoning abilities. In law school you will take such classes as legal writing and research, contracts, constitutional law, and property. You should also take courses in intellectual property law, which are necessary for any type of patent lawyer. You will graduate from law school with a juris doctor (J.D.) degree or a bachelor of laws (LL.B.) degree.

## Certification or Licensing

To practice any type of law, you must pass the bar exam of the state where you intend to practice. To qualify for the bar exam in most states, you must usually have a college degree as well as a law degree from a law school accredited by the American Bar Association (ABA). Many find these requirements are tough enough, but would-be patent lawyers have a much longer and harder road to travel before they can practice. First, all patent attorneys must pass another bar exam specific to patent law and given by the U.S. Patent and Trademark Office. Patent attorneys must then also prove that they have at least an undergraduate degree in one of the scientific fields that has been approved by the U.S. Patent and Trademark Office.

## Other Requirements

While scientific aptitude and knowledge are clearly important for achieving success in this field, verbal skills tend to be at least as important as the more analytic, scientific ones. "When you're dealing with someone who has invented a specific technology," Lawrence Foster remarks, "you're dealing with probably one of the most knowledgeable people in this particular scientific area in the whole world." While just communicating with the inventor may take all your skill and scientific background, the even greater challenge often comes when you have to communicate that specialized and technical knowledge to a judge who may have no scientific training. "As a biotech patent attorney, your job often requires translating from the most specialized to the most general kinds of language," Foster sums up. "That takes just as much verbal skill as it does scientific knowledge."

## EXPLORING

Since biotechnology patent law combines the areas of science and law, there are a number of ways you can explore this field. To investigate the law aspect of this career, try to get a part-time job or internship with a law office in your area. You will probably be doing tasks such as filing papers, photocopying, and answering phones, but this experience will give you an idea of what working in a law office is like. If you can't find such a job, try locating a lawyer in your area with whom you could do an information interview. Even if the lawyer is not a biotechnology patent lawyer, he or she may be able to give you some insights into the practice of law and the experience of law school.

To explore the science aspects of this career, consider joining a science or engineering club at your school. Ask your science teacher about any contacts he or she might have with scientists at the university level. You may be able to set up an information interview with a scientist working on or having completed a Ph.D. Find out what this person likes about the field and get any advice he or she may offer to a young scientist.

## EMPLOYERS

Many biotechnology patent attorneys work for law firms that focus on biotechnology patent law or intellectual property law, although some practice at firms that offer a wider range of legal specialties. Other lawyers practice at larger biotechnology corporations that hire their own in-house counsels, or at the U.S. Patent and Trademark Office itself. For all biotechnology patent lawyers, however, the work environment tends to be formal and often intense, since the amount of money at issue in biotechnology patent suits is usually substantial. Biotechnology patent law tends to be most active in areas where the industry itself is strong; currently, these areas include Boston, San Francisco, San Diego, and Washington, D.C.

## STARTING OUT

Internships and clerkships are often good ways to gain experience and enter the law field. Like other patent lawyers, you may want to apply for a clerkship in the U.S. Court of Appeals for the Federal Court in Washington, D.C. To gain a clerkship, you should write to the judge while you are still in law school. Another option is to get a job at the U.S. Patent and Trademark Office. Finally, many people are recruited by law firms right out of law school. Your law school should have a career services office as well as offer you professional contacts through alumni that help you find a position.

## ADVANCEMENT

For biotechnology patent lawyers who excel at combining verbal and scientific skills, advancement can be rapid and exciting. It is not uncommon for lawyers with Ph.D.'s in genetic engineering or related fields to find themselves flooded with clients. The most successful of these lawyers can hope to advance to partner positions at their firms or even to establish a sufficient client base with which to start their own firms.

## EARNINGS

In the law field, salaries tend to increase in predictable increments as the lawyer gains in experience and seniority. According to the U.S. Department of Labor (DOL), the median annual income for all lawyers was $113,240 in 2009. The middle 50 percent earned salaries between $76,270 and $166,400. The lowest paid 10 percent made less than $55,270. Higher salaries are generally found in major urban areas at large firms with 75 or more lawyers.

Because of the advanced training required and the high stakes of the biotech industry, biotechnology patent attorneys tend to earn about $10,000 to $20,000 more a year than their peers at each rung of this ladder. For example, while a starting attorney may earn about $70,000, a starting biotechnology patent attorney would make as much as $90,000. Other factors can also influence these numbers, however, including the degrees held by lawyers, the size of the firm, and the geographic location of the firm.

Most lawyers receive standard benefits from their employers, including health insurance and retirement plans.

## WORK ENVIRONMENT

Generally, there is a heavy workload with this career, and stress is part of the job. Because there are still relatively few biotech patent lawyers, successful ones can find themselves in especially high demand, and keeping hours down to an even remotely reasonable number can be a challenge. However, even this negative aspect has its upside, since biotech patent lawyers entering the field in the next few years should find plenty of demand for their talents. Some travel may be involved in the work, and, of course, biotechnology patent lawyers must be able to work with a variety of people. In addition, these lawyers often have the benefit of having their intellectual curiosity satisfied by their work.

## OUTLOOK

The DOL predicts that employment for all lawyers to grow about as fast as the average for all careers through 2018, although competition for the best jobs will be intense. Biotechnology patent attorneys should have a good future based on several factors. Because the legislation allowing for the patenting of biological organisms has only been in existence since the early 1980s, the pool of trained biotech patent attorneys is still relatively small. Currently, many of the practicing biotechnology patent attorneys came to the field as a second career once they had already obtained their scientific training. As Lawrence Foster points out, "It wasn't really until the mid-1990s that college students began to choose and pursue careers as biotechnology patent attorneys." In addition, the growing demand for sophisticated biotechnology tools has spurred growth in this industry. Protecting the rights of clients with new ideas and products and protecting the rights of clients who currently have patents should create many job opportunities for these specialty lawyers.

As with other law fields, the development of biotech patent law is closely tied to the development of the industry it supports. In recent years, many biotechnology corporations have begun merging with and buying out smaller companies, resulting in fewer and larger companies. If this development continues, more companies will be large enough to hire their own in-house counsels.

## FOR MORE INFORMATION

*For information on all areas of law, law schools, the bar exam, and career guidance, contact*
   **American Bar Association**
   321 North Clark Street
   Chicago, IL 60654-7598
   Tel: 312-988-5000
   E-mail: askaba@abanet.org
   http://www.abanet.org

*For more information on the specialty of intellectual property law, contact*

**American Intellectual Property Law Association**
241 18th Street South, Suite 700
Arlington, VA 22202-3419
Tel: 703-415-0780
E-mail: aipla@aipla.org
http://www.aipla.org

*Visit the association's Web site for information on member schools, the* Journal of Legal Education, *and links to other legal organizations.*

**Association of American Law Schools**
1201 Connecticut Avenue, NW, Suite 800
Washington, DC 20036-2717
Tel: 202-296-8851
E-mail: aals@aals.org
http://www.aals.org

*For career information, including articles and books on the biotechnology industry, contact*

**Biotechnology Industry Organization**
1201 Maryland Avenue, SW, Suite 900
Washington, DC 20024-2149
Tel: 202-962-9200
E-mail: info@bio.org
http://www.bio.org

*For information on the LSAT and law schools, contact*

**Law School Admission Council**
662 Penn Street, Box 40
Newtown, PA 18940-2176
Tel: 215-968-1001
http://www.lsac.org

*Visit the association's Web site for information on patent law, job listings, and membership for students preparing to become patent lawyers or patent agents.*

**National Association of Patent Practitioners**
3356 Station Court
Lawrenceville, GA 30044-5674
Tel: 800-216-9588
http://www.napp.org

*To learn more about patents and trademarks, contact*
**U.S. Patent and Trademark Office**
Director of U.S. Patent and Trademark Office
PO Box 1450
Alexandria, VA 22313-1450
Tel: 800-786-9199
E-mail: usptoinfo@uspto.gov
http://www.uspto.gov

# Botanists

## QUICK FACTS

**School Subjects**
Agriculture
Biology
Earth science

**Personal Skills**
Helping/teaching
Technical/scientific

**Work Environment**
Indoors and outdoors
Primarily one location

**Minimum Education Level**
Bachelor's degree

**Salary Range**
$33,254 to $59,180 to
$107,670+

**Certification or Licensing**
None available

**Outlook**
Faster than the average

**DOT**
041

**GOE**
02.03.02, 02.03.03

**NOC**
2121

**O*NET-SOC**
19-1013.00, 19-1020.01

## OVERVIEW

*Botanists* study all different aspects of plant life, from cellular structure to reproduction, to how plants are distributed, to how rainfall or other conditions affect them, and more. Botany is an integral part of modern science and industry, with diverse applications in agriculture, agronomy (soil and crop science), conservation, manufacturing, forestry, horticulture, and other areas. Botanists work for the government, in research and teaching institutions, and for private industry. The primary task of botanists is research and applied research. Nonresearch jobs in testing and inspection, or as lab technicians/ technical assistants, also are available. Botany is an extremely diverse field with many specialties.

## HISTORY

Plant science is hundreds of years old. The invention of microscopes in the 1600s was very important to the development of modern botany. Microscopes allowed minute study of plant anatomy and cells and led to considerable research in the field. It was in the 1600s that people started using words like *botanographist* or *botanologist*, for one who describes plants.

In the 1700s, Carolus Linnaeus, a Swedish botanist and *taxonomist* (one who identifies, names, and classifies plants) was an important figure. He came up with the two-name (genus and species) system for describing plants that is still used today. In all, Linnaeus wrote more than 180 works on plants, plant diseases, and related subjects.

A botanist (*right*) and a plant genetic resources specialist collect plant samples. *(Alejandro Balaguer, Agricultural Research Service, USDA)*

In Austria, during the 19th century, monk Gregor Johann Mendel did the first experiments in hybridization. He experimented on garden peas and other plants to figure out why organisms inherit the traits they do. His work is the basis for 20th and 21st century work in plant and animal genetics. As interest in botany grew, botanical gardens became popular in Europe and North America.

Botany is a major branch of biology; the other is zoology. Today, studies in botany reach into many areas of biology, including genetics, biophysics, and other specialized studies. It has taken on particular urgency as a potential source of help for creating new drugs to fight disease, meeting food needs of developing countries, and battling environmental problems.

## THE JOB

Research and applied research are the primary tasks of botanists. Literally every aspect of plant life is studied: cell structure, anatomy, heredity, reproduction, and growth; how plants are distributed on the earth; how rainfall, climate, soil, elevation, and other conditions affect plants; and how humans can put plants to better use. In most cases, botanists work at a specific problem or set of problems in their research. For example, they may develop new varieties of crops that will better resist disease. Some botanists focus on a specific type of plant species, such as fungi (mycology), or plants that are native to a specific area, such as a forest or prairie. A botanist working in private industry, for example, for a food or drug company, may focus on the development of new products, testing and inspection, regulatory compliance, or other areas.

Research takes place in laboratories, experiment stations (research sites found at many universities), botanical gardens, and other facilities. Powerful microscopes and special mounting, staining, and preserving techniques may be used in this sort of research.

Some botanists, particularly those working in conservation or ecological areas, also go out into the field. They inventory species, help re-create lost or damaged ecosystems, or direct pollution cleanup efforts.

Nonresearch jobs in testing and inspection or as lab technicians/technical assistants for universities, museums, government agencies, parks, manufacturing companies, botanical gardens, and other facilities also are available.

Botany is an extremely diverse field with many specialties. *Ethnobotanists* study the use of plant life by a particular culture, people, or ethnic group to find medicinal uses of certain plants. Study of traditional Native American medicinal uses of plants is an example. (For more information, see the article Ethnoscientists.)

*Forensic botanists* collect and analyze plant material found at crime scenes.

*Forest ecologists* focus on forest species and their habitats, such as forest wetlands. Related studies include forest genetics and forest economics. Jobs in forestry include work in managing, maintaining, and improving forest species and environments.

*Mycologists* study fungi and apply their findings in agriculture, medicine, and industry for development of drugs, medicines, molds, and yeasts. They may specialize in research and development in a field such as antibiotics.

*Toxicologists* study the effect of toxic substances on organisms, including plants. Results of their work may be used in regulatory action, product labeling, and other areas. (For more information, see the article Toxicologists.)

Other botanical specialists include *morphologists*, who study macroscopic plant forms and life cycles; *palyologists*, who study pollen and spores; *pteridologists*, who study ferns and other related plants; *bryologists*, who study mosses and similar plants; and *lichenologists*, who study lichens, which are dual organisms made of both alga and fungus.

# REQUIREMENTS

## High School

To prepare for a career in botany, high school students can explore their interests by taking biology, doing science projects involving plants, and working during summers or school holidays for a nursery, park, or similar operation. College prep courses in chemistry, physics, biology, mathematics, English, and foreign language are a good idea because educational requirements for professional botanists are high. Nonresearch jobs (test and inspection professionals, lab technicians, technical assistants) require at least a bachelor's degree in a biological science or botany; research and teaching positions usually require at least a master's degree or even a doctorate.

## Postsecondary Training

At the undergraduate level, there are numerous programs for degrees in botany or biology (which includes studies in both botany and zoology). The master's level and above usually involves a specialized degree. One newer degree is conservation biology, which focuses on the conservation of specific plant and animal communities. The University of Wisconsin-Madison (http://www.nelson.wisc.edu/education/programs/graduate-degrees/cbsd/overview.html) has one of the biggest programs in the United States. Another key school is Yale University's School of Forestry and Environmental Studies (http://environment.yale.edu), which offers degrees in areas such as natural resource management.

## Other Requirements

Botanists chose their profession because of their love for plants, gardening, and nature. They need patience, an exploring spirit, the ability to work well alone or with other people, good writing and other communication skills, and tenacity.

# EXPLORING

The Botanical Society of America (BSA) suggests that high school students take part in science fairs and clubs and get summer jobs with parks, nurseries, farms, experiment stations, labs, camps, florists, or landscape architects. Hobbies like camping, photography, and computers are useful, too, says the BSA. Additionally, the BSA offers a membership category for amateur botanists. Tour a botanical garden in your area and talk to staff. You can also get information by contacting national associations. For example, visit the Botanical Society of America's Web site (http://www.botany.org) to read a brochure on careers in botany.

## EMPLOYERS

Botanists find employment in the government, in research and teaching institutions, and in private industry. Local, state, and federal agencies, including the Department of Agriculture, Environmental Protection Agency, Public Health Service, Biological Resources Discipline, and the National Aeronautics and Space Administration employ botanists. Countless colleges and universities have botany departments and conduct botanical research. In private industry, botanists work for agribusiness, biotechnology, biological supply, chemical, environmental, food, lumber and paper, pharmaceutical, and petrochemical companies. Botanists also work for greenhouses, arboretums, herbariums, seed and nursery companies, and fruit growers.

## STARTING OUT

With a bachelor's degree, a botanist's first job may be as a technical assistant or technician for a lab. Those with a master's degree might get work on a university research project. Someone with a doctorate might get into research and development with a drug, pharmaceutical, or other manufacturer.

For some positions, contract work might be necessary before the botanist gains a full-time position. Contract work is work done on a per-project, or freelance, basis: You sign on for that one project, and then you move on. Conservation groups like The Nature Conservancy (TNC) hire hundreds of contract workers, including ecologists and botanists, each year to do certain work. Contract workers are especially in demand in the summer when there's a lot of biology inventory work to be done.

Opportunities for internships are available with local chapters of TNC. It's also possible to volunteer. Contact the Student Conservation Association (SCA) for volunteer opportunities. (Contact information for the SCA and TNC can be found at the end of this article.) Land trusts are also good places to check for volunteer work.

The Internet is also a good place to seek out information on botany-related positions. Both the Botanical Society of America (http://www.botany.org) and the American Society of Plant Biologists (http://www.aspb.org) provide job listings at their Web sites.

# ADVANCEMENT

Federal employees generally move up the ranks after gaining a certain number of hours of experience and obtaining advanced degrees. The Botanical Society of America, whose membership primarily comes from universities, notes that key steps for advancing in university positions include producing quality research, publishing a lot, and obtaining advanced degrees. Advancing in the private sector depends on the individual employer. Whatever the botanist can do to contribute to the bottom line, such as making breakthroughs in new product development, improving growing methods, and creating better test and inspection methods, will probably help the botanist advance in the company.

# EARNINGS

According to the U.S. Department of Labor (DOL), the median annual salary of soil and plant scientists was $59,180 in 2009. The lowest paid 10 percent (which generally included those just starting out in the field) earned less than $34,930, while the highest paid 10 percent made $107,670 or more per year. According to the National Association of Colleges and Employers, in July 2009 graduates with a bachelor's degree in biological and life sciences received average starting salary offers of $33,254 a year. Botanists working for the federal government earned mean salaries of $72,792 a year in 2009. Benefits vary but usually include paid holidays and vacations, and health insurance.

# WORK ENVIRONMENT

Botanists work in a wide variety of settings, some of them very pleasant: greenhouses, botanical gardens, and herbariums, for example. A botanist working for an environmental consultant or conservation organization may spend a lot of time outdoors, rain or shine. Some botanists interact with the public, such as in a public park or greenhouse, sharing their enthusiasm for the field. Other botanists spend their days in a lab, poring over specimens and writing up the results of their research.

As scientists, botanists need to be focused, patient, and determined. A botanist needs to believe in what he or she is doing and keep at a project until it's completed satisfactorily. The ability to work on one's own is important, but few scientists work in a vacuum. They cooperate with others, share the results of their work orally and in writing, and, particularly in private industry, may need to explain what they're doing in layman's terms.

Some research spans many hours and even years of work. At times, research botanists deeply involved with a project put in a lot of overtime. In exchange, they may be able to work fewer hours other weeks, depending on the specific employer. Botanists performing fieldwork also might have some flexibility of hours. In private industry, the workweek is likely to be a standard 35 to 40 hours.

Educational requirements for botanists are high and so much of the work involves research. Therefore it is important to be a good scholar and enjoy digging for answers.

## OUTLOOK

Employment for biological scientists, not otherwise classified (a category that includes botanists), is expected to grow faster than the average for all occupations through 2018, according to the DOL. Botanists will be needed to help meet growing environmental, conservation, pharmaceutical, and similar demands. However, budget cuts and a large number of graduates have made competition for jobs strong. Government employment opportunities should stay strong, but will depend in part on the continued health of the national economy. Federal budget cuts may jeopardize some projects and positions. Experts say the outlook is best for those with an advanced degree.

## FOR MORE INFORMATION

*For information on forensic biology, contact*
**American Academy of Forensic Sciences**
410 North 21st Street
Colorado Springs, CO 80904-2712
Tel: 719-636-1100
http://www.aafs.org

*The Education section of the institute's Web site has information on a number of careers in biology.*
**American Institute of Biological Sciences**
1444 I Street, NW, Suite 200
Washington, DC 20005-6535
Tel: 202-628-1500
http://www.aibs.org

*For general information about plant biology, contact*
**American Society of Plant Biologists**
http://www.aspb.org

*For comprehensive information on careers, contact*
**Botanical Society of America**
PO Box 299
St. Louis, MO 63166-0299
Tel: 314-577-9566
E-mail: bsa-manager@botany.org
http://www.botany.org

*For information about internships with state chapters or at TNC headquarters, contact*
**The Nature Conservancy (TNC)**
4245 North Fairfax Drive, Suite 100
Arlington, VA 22203-1606
Tel: 800-628-6860
http://www.nature.org

*To learn about volunteer positions in natural resource management, contact*
**Student Conservation Association**
689 River Road
PO Box 550
Charlestown, NH 03603-0550
Tel: 603-543-1700
E-mail: ask-us@thesca.org
http://www.thesca.org

*This government agency manages more than 535 national wildlife refuges. The service's Web site has information on volunteer opportunities, careers, and answers to frequently asked questions.*
**U.S. Fish & Wildlife Service**
U.S. Department of the Interior
1849 C Street, NW
Washington, DC 20240-0001
Tel: 800-344-9453
http://www.fws.gov

# Cytotechnologists

## QUICK FACTS

**School Subjects**
Biology
Chemistry

**Personal Skills**
Helping/teaching
Technical/scientific

**Work Environment**
Primarily indoors
Primarily one location

**Minimum Education Level**
Bachelor's degree

**Salary Range**
$37,540 to $55,140 to
$75,960+

**Certification or Licensing**
Required by certain states

**Outlook**
Faster than the average

**DOT**
078

**GOE**
14.05.01

**NOC**
3211

**O*NET-SOC**
29-2011.02

## OVERVIEW

*Cytotechnologists* are laboratory specialists who study cells under microscopes, searching for cell abnormalities such as changes in color, shape, or size that might indicate the presence of disease. Cytotechnologists may also assist pathologists in the collection of body cells from various body sites, prepare slides, keep records, file reports, and consult with coworkers and pathologists. Most cytotechnologists work in private medical laboratories or in the laboratories of hospitals or research institutions.

## HISTORY

The cytotechnology field is only slightly less than 70 years old. It began in the 1940s, more than 10 years after Dr. George N. Papanicolaou, a Greek-American physician, developed a procedure for early diagnosis of cancer of the cervix in 1928, now known as the "Pap smear." This test involved collecting cell samples by scraping the cervixes of female patients, placing them on glass slides, staining them, and examining them under a microscope to detect cell differences and abnormalities. As the value of the test became more widely accepted, the demand for trained personnel to read the Pap smears grew, and the career of cytotechnologist was born. This field has expanded to include the examination of other cell specimens.

## THE JOB

Cytotechnologists primarily examine prepared slides of body cells by viewing them through a microscope. In any single slide there may be more than 100,000 cells so it is important that cytotechnologists be patient, thorough, and accurate when performing their job. They are required to study the slides and examine cell growth patterns, looking for abnormal patterns or changes in a cell's color, shape, or size that might indicate the presence of disease. In addition to analyzing Pap smears, they interpret specimens taken from the lung, breast, central nervous system, gastrointestinal tract, bladder, body cavities, liver, lymph nodes, thyroid, and salivary glands.

While most cytotechnologists spend the majority of their workday in the laboratory, some might assist doctors at patients' bedsides collecting cell samples from the respiratory and urinary systems, as well as the gastrointestinal tract. They might also assist physicians with bronchoscopes and with needle aspirations, a process that uses very fine needles to suction cells from many locations within the body. Once the cells are collected, cytotechnologists may prepare the slides for microscope examination. In some laboratories, cell preparation is done by medical technicians known as *cytotechnicians*.

Cytotechnologists are often responsible for keeping records and filing reports. Although they usually work independently in the lab, they often share lab space and must consult with coworkers, supervisors, and pathologists regarding their findings. Most cytotechnologists work for private firms that are hired by physicians to evaluate medical tests, but they may also work for hospitals or university research institutions.

## REQUIREMENTS

### High School
Biology, chemistry, and other science courses are essential if you want to become a cytotechnologist. In addition, math, English, and computer literacy classes are also important. You should also take the courses necessary to fulfill the entrance requirements of the college or university you plan to attend.

### Postsecondary Training
There are two options for becoming a cytotechnologist. The first involves earning a bachelor's degree in biology, life sciences, or a related field, then entering a one-year, postbaccalaureate certificate program offered by an accredited hospital or university.

The second option involves transferring into a cytotechnology program during your junior or senior year of college. Students on this track earn a bachelor of science degree in cytotechnology. In both cases, you would earn a college degree and complete at least one year of training devoted to cytotechnology.

The courses you will take include chemistry, biology, and math. Some programs also require their students to take business and computer classes as well.

There are currently 33 accredited programs in cytotechnology. Visit the Web site (http://www.caahep.org/Find-An-Accredited-Program) of the Commission on Accreditation of Allied Health Education Programs for a complete list of programs.

**Certification or Licensing**

Cytotechnology graduates (from either degree programs or certificate programs) may register for the certification examination given by the Board of Registry of the American Society for Clinical Pathology. Most states require cytotechnologists to be certified, and most employers insist that new employees be certified. Certification is usually a requirement for advancement in the field.

A number of states also require that personnel working in laboratories be licensed. It will be necessary for you to check the licensing requirements of the state in which you hope to work. The state's department of health or board of occupational licensing can provide you with this information.

It is important that practicing cytotechnologists remain current with new ideas, techniques, and medical discoveries. Many continuing education programs are offered to help the professional remain current in the field of cytotechnology.

**Other Requirements**

If you wish to enter the field of cytotechnology you should be detail oriented, a good observer, and able to make decisions. You should enjoy working alone, but you must also have the ability to work as a team member. It is essential that you are able to follow directions and have the ability to concentrate. Good writing, reporting, and organizational skills are also important. Cytotechnologists are often expected to sit at a stationary laboratory bench for long periods of time.

# EXPLORING

Participate in science clubs and competitions that help you become familiar with microscopes and allow you to practice making slides. Ask a science teacher or counselor to help you contact museums that are involved in research. These museums may let students view slide collections and see what goes on behind the scenes. Working with and solving puzzles is also recommended since cytotechnologists perform similar actions when studying slides.

Volunteer or apply for part-time work at hospitals or independent laboratories to get experience in health care settings.

Ask your counselor or science teacher to arrange an information interview with a cytotechnologist.

## EMPLOYERS

The majority of cytotechnologists are employed by private medical laboratories hired by physicians to evaluate medical tests. Others work for hospitals, nursing homes, public health facilities, or university research institutions, while some may be employed by federal and state governments.

## STARTING OUT

Some universities and teaching hospitals have internship programs that can result in job offers upon graduation. Recruiters often visit universities and teaching hospitals in the months prior to a graduation in an effort to recruit cytotechnologists. Professional journals and large metropolitan newspapers often have classified ads that list opportunities for employment. Many university and teaching hospitals have a placement service that helps their graduates obtain employment upon graduation.

## ADVANCEMENT

Some cytotechnologists who work in larger labs may advance to supervisory positions. This type of advancement may be limited in smaller labs, however. Entering the teaching field and directing classes or supervising research may be another career advancement move. Some experienced cytotechnologists, along with other medical personnel, open their own laboratories. Obtaining additional education or training can open the door to other careers in the medical field.

## EARNINGS

Salaries are determined by the experience and education of the cytotechnologist and by the type and size of employer. For example, federal government employees are generally paid a higher salary than those working in the private sector, and cytotechnologists working in private clinics earn slightly more than those working in hospitals.

The U.S. Department of Labor (DOL) reports the median yearly income of medical and clinical laboratory technologists (a group that includes cytotechnologists) was $55,140 in 2009. The lowest paid 10 percent, which typically includes those just beginning in the field, earned less than $37,540. The highest paid 10 percent made more than $75,960 annually.

The American Society for Clinical Pathology reports that cyto-technologists earned the following median annual salaries by employer in 2008: private clinic, $62,400; and hospital, $57,200.

Benefits such as vacation time, sick leave, insurance, and other fringe benefits vary by employer, but are usually consistent with other full-time health care workers.

## WORK ENVIRONMENT

Cytotechnologists usually work independently in a well-lighted laboratory examining slides under the microscope. Often this involves sitting at a workstation for a considerable length of time and requires intense concentration. Some cytotechnologists might assist other medical personnel with the direct collection of cell samples from patients. This type of work requires interacting directly with people who are ill or who may be concerned about their health and the test results. Cytotechnologists do not necessarily work nine-to-five hours. Daily schedules and shifts may vary according to the size of the laboratory and medical facility.

## OUTLOOK

The DOL predicts that employment for all medical and clinical technologists will grow faster than the average for all careers through 2018. Employment will grow fastest in medical and diagnostic laboratories, offices of physicians, and other ambulatory health care services. Advances in technology have made many new diagnostic tests possible, but advances in technology have also caused much automation to take place in the laboratory. So, while there are new tests for the cytotechnologist to perform, there are also fewer old tests that need the cytotechnologist's expert handling. However, it is important to note that government regulations currently limit the number of slides cytotechnologists may work with each day, adding to demand for workers in this field.

# FOR MORE INFORMATION

*For information on cytotechnology careers, accredited schools, and employment opportunities, contact the following organizations:*

**American Society for Clinical Pathology**
33 West Monroe, Suite 1600
Chicago, IL 60603-5308
Tel: 800-267-2727
E-mail: info@ascp.org
http://www.ascp.org

**American Society for Cytotechnology**
1500 Sunday Drive, Suite 102
Raleigh, NC 27607-5151
Tel: 800-948-3947
E-mail: info@asct.com
http://www.asct.com

**American Society of Cytopathology**
100 West 10th Street, Suite 605
Wilmington, DE 19801-6604
Tel: 302-543-6583
E-mail: asc@cytopathology.org
http://www.cytopathology.org

*For information on accredited programs, contact*

**Commission on Accreditation of Allied Health Education Programs**
1361 Park Street
Clearwater, FL 33756-6039
Tel: 727-210-2350
E-mail: mail@caahep.org
http://www.caahep.org

# Ecologists

## OVERVIEW

Ecology is the study of the interconnections between organisms (plants, animals) and the physical environment. It links biology, which includes both zoology (the study of animals) and botany (the study of plants), with physical sciences such as geology and paleontology. Thus, *ecologist* is a broad name for any of a number of different biological or physical scientists concerned with the study of plants or animals within their environment.

## HISTORY

Much of the science that ecologists use is not new. The ancient Greeks recorded their observations of natural history many centuries ago. However, linking together the studies of life and the physical environment is fairly new. Ernst von Haeckel, a German biologist, first defined the term ecology in 1866. Like many scientists of his time, he grappled with Charles Darwin's theory of evolution based on natural selection. This theory said that those species of plants and animals that were best adapted to their environment would survive. Although Haeckel did not agree with Darwin, he and many other scientists grew fascinated with the links between living things and their physical environment. At that time, very important discoveries in geology proved that many forms of plants and animals had once existed but had died out. Fossils showed startlingly unfamiliar plant types, for example, as well as prehistoric animal remains that no one had ever imagined existed. (Before such discoveries, people assumed that the species they saw all around them had always existed.) Realization that there were important

An aquatic ecologist bottles samples of river water to test for the presence of mercury, a toxic heavy metal. *(Mike Tripp,* The News Leader/AP *Photo)*

connections between living things and their physical environment was a key step in the development of the science of ecology.

Like most of the other environmental careers, the professional field of ecology did not really grow popular until the late 1960s and early 1970s. Before then, some scientists and others had tried to warn the public about the ill effects of industrialization, unchecked natural resource consumption, overpopulation, spoiling of wilderness areas, and other thoughtless misuse of the environment. But not until the years after World War II (with growing use of radiation and of pesticides and other chemicals, soaring industrial and automobile pollution, and increasing discharge into waterways) did widespread public alarm about the environment grow. By this time, many feared it was too late. Heavy municipal and industrial discharge into Lake Erie, for example, made it unable to sustain life as before.

In response, the U.S. government passed a series of hard-hitting environmental laws during the 1960s and 1970s. To become compliant with these laws, companies and municipalities began to seek professionals who understood the problems and could help take steps to remedy them. Originally they drew professionals from many existing fields, such as geologists, sanitary engineers, biologists, and chemists. These professionals may not have studied environmental problems as such at school, but they were able to apply the science they knew to the problems at hand.

To some extent, this continues to be true today. Many people working on environmental problems still come from general science or engineering backgrounds. Recently, however, there has been a trend toward specialization. Students in fields such as biology, chemistry, engineering, law, urban planning, and communications can obtain degrees with specialization in the environment. An ecologist today can either have a background in traditional biological or physical sciences or have studied these subjects specifically in the context of environmental problems.

## THE JOB

The main unit of study in ecology is the ecosystem. Ecosystems are communities of plants and animals within a given habitat that provide the necessary means of survival, including food and water. Ecosystems are defined by such physical conditions as climate, altitude, latitude, and soil and water characteristics. Examples include forests, tundra, savannas (grasslands), and rainforests.

There are many complex and delicate interrelationships within an ecosystem. For example, green plants use the energy of sunlight to make carbohydrates, fats, and proteins; some animals eat these plants and acquire part of the energy of the carbohydrates, fats, and proteins; other animals eat these animals and acquire a smaller part of that energy. Cycles of photosynthesis, respiration, and nitrogen fixation continuously recycle the chemicals of life needed to support the ecosystem. Anything that disrupts these cycles, such as droughts, or the pollution of air or water, can disrupt the delicate workings of the entire ecosystem.

Therefore a primary concern of ecologists today is to study and attempt to find solutions for disruptions in various ecosystems. Increasingly an area of expertise is the reconstruction of ecosystems—that is, the restoration of ecosystems that are destroyed or almost completely destroyed because of pollution, overuse of land, or other action.

A key area of work for ecologists is in land and water conservation. They help to restore damaged land and water as well as to preserve wild areas for the future. Understanding the links between organisms and their physical environments can be invaluable in such efforts.

Let us take an example to see how this works. Imagine that there is a large pond at the edge of a town. A woman out jogging one day notices that hundreds of small, dead fish have washed up at the edge of the pond; a "fish kill," in environmental language. Clearly something is wrong, but what? A nearby factory discharges its wastewater into the pond. Is there something new in the wastewater that killed the fish? Or did something else kill the fish? A professional who understands the fish, the habitat (the pond), the possible reasons for the fish kill, and the potential solutions clearly would be useful here.

This is also true for environmental planning and resource management. Planning involves studying and reporting the impact of an action on the environment. For example, how might the construction of a new federal highway affect the surrounding ecosystem? A planning team may go to the site to view the physical geography and environment, the plants, and the animals. It also may recommend alternative actions that will have less damaging effects.

Resource management means determining what resources already exist and working to use them wisely. Professionals may build databases cataloging the plants, animals, and physical characteristics of a given area. They also may report on what can be done to ensure that the ecosystem can continue to sustain itself in the future. If an ecosystem has been completely destroyed, ecologists can help reconstruct it, getting the physical environment back up to par and reintroducing the species that used to live there.

Ecologists work in many areas of specialization. *Limnologists* study freshwater ecology; *hydrogeologists* focus on water on or below the surface of the earth; *paleontologists* study the remains of ancient life-forms in the form of fossils; *geomorphologists* study the origin of landforms and their changes; and *geochemists* study the chemistry of the earth, including the effect of pollution on the earth's chemistry. Other specialties include endangered species biologist and wetlands ecologist.

## REQUIREMENTS

### High School
If you are interested in becoming an ecologist, you should take a college preparatory curriculum while in high school. Classes that will be of particular benefit include earth science, biology, chemistry, English, and math. Because computers are so often involved in various aspects of research and documentation, you should also take computer science courses.

### Postsecondary Training
A bachelor of science degree is the minimum degree required for nonresearch jobs, which include testing and inspection. A master's

degree is necessary for jobs in applied research or management. A Ph.D. generally is required to advance in the field, including into administrative positions.

If you can only pursue one undergraduate major, it should be in the basic sciences: biology, botany, zoology, chemistry, physics, or geology. At the master's degree level, natural resource management, ecology, botany, conservation biology, and forestry studies are useful.

### Certification or Licensing

The Ecological Society of America offers professional certification at three levels: associate ecologist, ecologist, and senior ecologist. A candidate's certification level will depend on the amount of education and professional experience he or she has. The society encourages certification as a way to enhance ecologists' professional standing in society.

### Other Requirements

Ecologists should appreciate and respect nature, and they must also be well versed in scientific fundamentals. Ecologists frequently, but not always, are naturally idealistic. They should be able to work with other people on a team and to express their special knowledge to the other people on the team, who may have different areas of specialization.

## EXPLORING

You can seek more information about ecology from guidance counselors and professional ecologists who work at nearby colleges, universities, and government agencies. An easy way for you to learn more about ecology is to study your own environment. Trips to a nearby pond, forest, or park over the course of several months will provide opportunities to observe and collect data. Science teachers and local park service or arboretum personnel can also offer you guidance.

## EMPLOYERS

By far the majority of land and water conservation jobs (about 75 percent) are in the public sector. This includes the federal government, the largest employer. The Bureau of Land Management, the U.S. Fish and Wildlife Service, the National Park Service, and the

U.S. Geological Survey are among the federal agencies that manage U.S. conservation. Other public sector opportunities are with states, regions, and towns. Opportunities in the private sector can be found with utilities, timber companies, and consulting firms. An additional area of employment is in teaching.

## STARTING OUT

Internships provide an excellent point of entry into this field. You can volunteer with such groups as the Student Conservation Association (SCA), which places people in resource management projects. Programs include three- to five-week summer internships for high school students. If you have already graduated from high school (and are over age 18), you can check with the SCA for internships in forest, wildlife, resource, and other agencies.

Another option is to contact a federal or local government agency directly about an internship. Many, including the Environmental Protection Agency, National Park Service, and Bureau of Land Management, have internship programs. Programs are more informal at the local level.

As for the private sector, an internship with a nonprofit organization may be possible. Such groups include the National Wildlife Federation and the Natural Resources Defense Council.

Entry-level ecologists also may take advantage of temporary or seasonal jobs to gain experience and establish crucial contacts in the field.

## ADVANCEMENT

Mid-level biological scientists may move to managerial positions within biology or to nontechnical administrative, sales, or managerial jobs. Ecologists with a Ph.D. may conduct independent research, advance into administrative positions, or teach at the college level, advancing from assistant professor to associate and tenured professorships.

## EARNINGS

Salaries for ecologists vary depending on such factors as their level of education, experience, area of specialization, and the organization for which they work. The U.S. Department of Labor (DOL) reported the median annual income of environmental scientists and specialists was $61,010 in 2009. Salaries ranged from less than $37,120 to $107,190 or more annually. Ecologists working for the federal government in 2009 earned average salaries of $93,700.

Federal agency jobs tend to pay more than state or local agency jobs. Private sector jobs tend to pay more than public sector jobs.

Benefits for ecologists depend on the employer; however, they usually include such items as health insurance, retirement or 401(k) plans, and paid vacation days.

## WORK ENVIRONMENT

Ecologists work in a variety of places, from wilderness areas to forests to mountain streams. Ecologists also might work in sewage treatment plants, spend their days in front of computers or in research laboratories, or find themselves testifying in court. A certain amount of idealism probably is useful, though not required. It takes more than just loving nature to be in this field; a person has to be good at scientific fundamentals. Ecologists might start out in the field collecting samples, making notes about animal habits, or doing other monitoring. They may need to be able to work as part of a team and express what they know in terms that everyone on the team can understand.

## OUTLOOK

Environmentally oriented jobs are expected to increase much faster than the average for all occupations through 2018, according to the DOL. Land and resource conservation jobs tend to be the most scarce, however, because of high popularity and tight budgets for such agencies. Opportunities should be best for ecologists who work for environmental consulting firms in the private sector. Those with advanced degrees will fare better than ecologists with only bachelor's degrees.

## FOR MORE INFORMATION

*For information on careers in the geosciences and a list of member societies, contact*
American Geological Institute
4220 King Street
Alexandria, VA 22302-1502
Tel: 703-379-2480
http://www.agiweb.org

*In addition to certification, the ESA offers a wide variety of publications, including* Issues in Ecology, Careers in Ecology, *and fact sheets about specific ecological concerns. For more information, contact*

**Ecological Society of America (ESA)**
1990 M Street, NW, Suite 700
Washington, DC 20036-3415
Tel: 202-833-8773
E-mail: esahq@esa.org
http://www.esa.org

*For information on internships, job opportunities, and student chapters, contact*

**National Wildlife Federation**
11100 Wildlife Center Drive
Reston, VA 20190-5362
Tel: 800-822-9919
http://www.nwf.org

*For information on student volunteer activities and programs, contact*

**Student Conservation Association**
689 River Road
PO Box 550
Charlestown, NH 03603-0550
Tel: 603-543-1700
E-mail: ask-us@thesca.org
http://www.thesca.org

## INTERVIEW

*Dr. Felicia Keesing is an ecologist and an associate professor of biology in the Department of Biology at Bard College in New York City. She discussed her career with the editors of* Careers in Focus: Biology.

**Q. What made you want to enter this career?**

**A.** I can't say I have a good answer to this question. I didn't decide to become an ecologist in anything that resembles a typical—and certainly not a recommended—way! I was actually studying paleontology in graduate school for the first couple of years and I got frustrated that I couldn't answer questions the way I wanted to. I'd actually never considered ecology, but I found an ecological question that interested me—whether small mammals play important roles in African savannas—and within a year I was doing ecological research in East Africa.

**Q. What is one thing that young people may not know about a career in ecology?**

**A.** Ecology is just as "hard" a science as any other. Most ecologists do a lot of math. Sorting out how ecological systems work is complicated and math is a crucial tool. Many ecologists also use chemistry or molecular biology in their work. I study the ecology of infectious diseases and we use molecular biology to figure out if animals are infected with particular pathogens.

**Q. Can you describe a day in your life on the job. What are your main research interests?**

**A.** My days are tremendously varied. I'm a college professor so during semesters, I spend a lot of time in the classroom or meeting with students. I try to keep one day a week to focus only on research, which sometimes means writing a paper and sometimes means getting into the lab to collect some data. When the school year ends, I immediately switch gears and start doing fieldwork.

I am interested in the ecological consequences of interactions among species. In Africa, I've been interested in how savannas function when large mammals like elephants and giraffes aren't there. In the United States, I study how the transmission of infectious diseases changes when species disappear.

**Q. What are the most important personal and professional qualities for ecologists? Educators?**

**A.** Of course, it's extremely important that you do what you are really interested in. I look forward to my job every day—the science and the teaching—and I wouldn't want to be doing anything else right now. I think my work is important, too, which makes it easier when I'm working hard.

On a more mundane level, I think there are two very important work habits for this job, and probably for any job. The first is efficiency. I have a lot of responsibilities and I try to juggle them as efficiently as possible. That means keeping my priorities clear so that I am aware of the tradeoffs I'm making when I spend time on any particular facet of my job.

But this brings me to the second work habit. I remind myself fairly frequently that any job worth doing is worth doing well. Not necessarily perfectly, but well.

**Q. What advice would you give to young people who are interested in becoming ecologists?**

**A.** Take lots of science classes, not just ecology, and take lots of math. Spend some time if you can with ecologists doing research so you have a sense of what ecologists really do. When you get to college, you should definitely take whatever opportunities you can to do research. This will help you learn the field and it will also make you stand out when you apply for jobs after graduation.

**Q. What is the future employment outlook for ecologists?**

**A.** There are lots of opportunities for people who want to teach science, including ecology, whether in K–12 education or at the college level. There are also many opportunities to apply ecological science in the real world through government agencies, nonprofit groups, and other organizations. These are likely to increase in number as we grapple with the complexities posed by human-induced environmental changes such as climate change.

# Ethnoscientists

## OVERVIEW

*Ethnoscientist* is a broad term that covers various specialties, such as ethnoarchaeology, ethnobiology, ethnomusicology, ethnoveterinary medicine, and ethnozoology. Ethnoscientists study a particular subject, usually a social or life science, (e.g., archaeology, biology, veterinary medicine, or zoology) from the perspective of one or more cultural groups.

Ethnoscientists are usually Western practitioners who are interested in exploring the knowledge, beliefs, traditions, and practices of cultures in nonindustrialized areas of the world, such as the Maoris of New Zealand, the Shona of south-central Africa, or the Inuit of Alaska. These cultures have unique, often undocumented, ways of perceiving, interacting with, and understanding each other and their environment. Ethnoscientists study these cultures to record and learn from their perspectives.

## HISTORY

Although the term is relatively new, ethnoscientific study has been around since people first began exploring the relationship between people and their environment, by studying music, language, biology, history, and all the elements that form societies and cultures.

Ethnoscience evolved as a subfield of ethnography, the study of cultural groups in the 19th century. The ethno- prefix became more widespread as the disciplines of ethnobotany, ethnobiology, and ethnoecology developed in about 1895, 1935, and 1954, respectively. Ethnohistory gained popularity in the 1930s and 1940s. Eugene Hunn, an anthropology professor with a specialization in

## Contributors to Ethnobiology and Ethnobotany

**Brent Berlin** (Ph.D., Stanford University, 1964) is well known for his collaborative field research in ethnobotany and medicinal plant use of the Mayans in Chiapas, Mexico, and Aguaruna ethnobiology in Peru. In 1973 he proposed "universals of ethnobotanical classification and nomenclature" that continue to guide research.

**Harold Conklin** (Ph.D., Yale University, 1955) wrote his dissertation on the Philippine Hanunoo tribe's knowledge of plants. His research helped define the field and establish high standards for the detailed ethnographic study of ethnobiology.

**Richard Evan Schultes** (Ph.D., Harvard University, 1941) initiated studies of the uses of hallucinogenic plants by Native American peoples and is well known for his documentation of the sophisticated knowledge Amazonian Indian tribes had of the chemical properties of plants. He is considered the father of ethnobotany.

ethnobiology at the University of Washington, says, "The term *ethnobotany* was first used to refer to museum studies of native peoples' uses of plants.

"Ethnoscience was a common label in the 1960s and 1970s for a particular focus in anthropology," Hunn continues. "This has evolved into cognitive anthropology, an emphasis within sociocultural anthropology and linguistic anthropology that focuses on cultural knowledge systems, particularly their linguistic expression."

Regarding the background of ethnoveterinary medicine, Evelyn Mathias, an independent consultant focusing on integrated livestock development, comments that interest in indigenous knowledge and ethnoveterinary medicine arose with the failure of many development projects that had regarded Western technology and approaches as superior and tried to use them in other cultures with little adaptation and modification. "Over the last two or three decades, it became increasingly obvious that this type of development is inappropriate and not sustainable. Scientists and development professionals have come to realize that local people's knowledge is a valuable resource for development and they have started to study and use it in projects."

Sound-recording devices, beginning with the phonograph, have enabled ethnoscientists to record and keep sounds, such as language (ethnolinguists) and music (ethnomusicologists). More recent innovations include multimedia technology, which, according to Hunn, "is being used more frequently to present the complex data of ethnobiology, which often must include images of plants and animals, recordings of sounds of animals, recordings of the pronunciation of native names, video footage of processing activities, etc."

## THE JOB

Ethnoscientists generally perform the same or similar duties as their counterparts in the traditional sciences, but from the perspective of the knowledge and belief systems of a particular indigenous group or culture. Not only do ethnoscientists conduct research in their particular area of study, but they immerse themselves in the culture and talk to the inhabitants to find out about, for example, the local knowledge and use (medicinally or otherwise) of plants (ethnobotanist or ethnopharmacologist), the local use of language (ethnolinguist), or the local use of implements, utensils, tools, or other items (ethnoarchaeologists). Ethnoscientists classify information based on traditional methods and concepts while at the same time drawing on linguistic and cognitive theories.

Because ethnoscientists study other cultural groups, they often have to travel to conduct their research and talk to the local people. Eugene Hunn says, "Summers or perhaps at other times when I can arrange to travel to do ethnobiological field research, I will go to Oaxaca, Mexico, Australia, or Alaska to visit villages where indigenous peoples still hunt, fish, gather, or farm their ancestral lands. With their permission and with their help, I collect plants, insects, and fungi, and observe birds, reptiles, and mammals—always with local guides who can explain to me what they call each organism and what importance each plant or bug might have for their lives. I spend a lot of time studying foreign languages and learning Latin names of plants and animals." It is important that ethnoscientists are not intrusive when conducting research. They must always remember that they are acting as observers rather than agents of change.

Hunn defines an *ethnobiologist* as "a scholar who studies what people in cultures around the world know about biology. Most often this means what they know about the plants and animals of their local environment. Ethnobiology includes *ethnobotany* (study of knowledge of local plants), *ethnozoology* (local animals), *ethnoentomology* (local insects), etc. Ethnobotany may focus on naming and classifying or on how plants are used, for example, for food, medicine, or construction materials. Ethnozoology could emphasize how animals are imagined in folklore or how domestic animals are cared for and utilized. Some ethnobiologists are archaeologists who analyze plant or animal remains for evidence of past use."

Hunn notes, "There are few, if any, jobs specifically for ethnobiologists, as it is a specialty that crosses the boundaries of typical academic disciplines." This also holds true for the other ethnosciences.

An ethnobiologist's primary duties are "to develop research proposals for funding that allow the researcher to travel to the field site for extended periods," explains Hunn. "An ethnobiologist collects voucher specimens (especially of plants, insects, fungi) in conjunction with recording the ethnographic information in the native language of the people of the community where the research takes place. There are ethical expectations that the ethnobiologist will publish his or her findings not only in academic journals and books but also in the local languages in a form readily accessible to the people of the study community and to the scholars of the host country (if outside the United States). Ethnobiologists in universities are expected to teach ethnobiology courses and to train students in ethnobiology."

In describing his typical day, Hunn reports, "Most of the time I work in my office preparing for classes, talking with students, reading other people's work, writing articles or books, sorting and analyzing my own data, and preparing grant proposals so that I can get out of the office and into the field, which is where I most like to be."

Evelyn Mathias explains ethnoveterinary medicine as the study of how people manage animal health care and production. "It covers everything herders and small farmers do and know to keep their animals healthy and productive." According to Mathias, there are two types of *ethnoveterinarians*. First there are the "local practitioners, such as herders, farmers, or healers, who use indigenous techniques to treat animals." And second are the "Western academics or development professionals who study and promote the use of indigenous techniques in agricultural development. Most of these are either veterinarians who are interested in traditional health care practices or anthropologists who study veterinary medicine."

Mathias's primary duties include doing laboratory research or a participatory research study in the field, collecting and summarizing literature, running a network on raising the awareness of the value of local knowledge, and doing project evaluations. Research entails documentation, laboratory and fieldwork, studying how to integrate local practices, and incorporating ethnoveterinary medicine into education programs.

Ethnobiologists and ethnoveterinarians account for only two of the many ethnoscience specialties. Given the multidisciplinary approach of the ethnosciences, there is great variance in definition, focus, and process among its many areas. But at the core of the ethnosciences is an immersion in other cultures and a desire to learn what is known, believed, and practiced by local inhabitants.

*Ethnobotanists* study the use and classification of indigenous plants by a particular cultural group. Plants may be used as drugs, food, cosmetics, clothing, building material, or as part of religious ceremonies. Ethnobotanists also evaluate whether these plants have more widespread value outside the region, especially in the case of medicinal plants.

Many wild plants can only be grown in their native environment—the Amazon rainforest, for example. Ethnobotanists must be especially aware that taking plants from their environment affects the entire ecosystem, including its human inhabitants.

Economic botany, the study of plants that are commercially important, is closely related to ethnobotany. *Ethnopharmacologists* conduct research that is similar to that of ethnobotanists. The difference is that ethnopharmacologists study indigenous plants focusing on their medicinal value and use only. Ethnopharmacologists examine current indigenous remedies derived from either plant or animal substances and look for ways to develop new and better drugs. Both ethnobotanists and ethnopharmacologists must be sure that the intellectual property rights of the local people are observed, and that they receive a share in whatever financial returns may result from knowledge or use elsewhere of indigenous plants.

*Ethnoecologists* focus on the knowledge and understanding that indigenous peoples have of their local ecology—that is, how they interact with their environment and other organisms.

Other ethnoscience specialties include ethnoarchaeology, ethnohistory, ethnolinguistics, ethnopsychiatry, and ethnomusicology.

## REQUIREMENTS

### High School

Sociology courses will teach you the basics of research methods and observation techniques. If your school offers any anthropology classes, be sure to take them. Learning another foreign language can be helpful if you conduct field research. The foreign language you take in high school may not be the one you will need later, but learning a second language should make it easier for you to learn others. History and art classes will expose you to the cultures of different peoples of the world.

Biology and chemistry will be useful if you're considering ethnobiology, ethnobotany, or ethnopharmacology. Evelyn Mathias recommends an assortment of classes if you're interested in ethnoveterinary medicine: geography, cultural studies, biology, zoology, botany, and agriculture. She stresses the importance of classes that highlight the value of cultural diversity. Math and computer classes are also helpful.

### Postsecondary Training

To teach at the university level, you will need a Ph.D. The particular field of study will depend on the line of work you want to enter. Anthropology classes, especially cultural anthropology, will be useful for study in just about any discipline. Classes in archaeology, linguistics, history, sociology, religion, and mythology can help prepare you to work with indigenous peoples. Some schools offer concentrations or courses in specific ethnosciences (e.g., ethnobiology).

If you want to pursue ethnoveterinary medicine, Mathias recommends getting a degree in a technical field, such as veterinary medicine, animal husbandry, biology, pharmacology, or botany, in addition to social science courses. To prepare for a career in ethnobotany, it is recommended that you get your degree in anthropology, botany, or pharmacology. Other important areas of study include chemistry, ecology, and medicine. According to Eugene Hunn, "Most professional ethnobiologists have doctoral degrees in anthropology or biology."

### Other Requirements

It is important that ethnoscientists possess an "openness and understanding for other cultures and the ability and willingness to learn from others and work with other peoples," notes Mathias. "Someone who has prejudices against other peoples and who believes that high-tech is the only solution possible" will not be suitable for this line of work. Many cultural groups of the world live lives that are far less technologically oriented than in the Western world. Ethnoscientists embrace those differences.

Ethnoscientists need a healthy curiosity and should enjoy research. They should be able to work independently and as part of a team.

Many ethnoscientists are away from home for extended periods and must be able to tolerate different climates, rustic accommodations, unusual foods, and demanding physical conditions. Adaptability is a key personality trait for ethnoscientists doing fieldwork.

## EXPLORING

A fascination with birds, bugs, snakes, fish, or plants is what got many of Eugene Hunn's ethnobiological colleagues started early.

"Later they realized that they weren't just interested in the plants and animals but in how those plants and animals fit into people's lives. So they studied anthropology or linguistics to better understand the human side of the equation."

Explore extracurricular, volunteer, or part-time opportunities that will give you some background experience in your field of interest. If it's ethnobotany, for example, look for a summer job working in a city park or with a local florist or nursery. If it's ethnoveterinary medicine, look for part-time or volunteer work at a veterinarian's office or animal shelter. To explore your interest in ethnozoology, work at a zoo. Museums offer a wealth of information on different cultures, including exhibits, reading materials, lectures, and workshops.

Take any opportunity offered you to travel, particularly to non-industrialized countries and more remote areas of the world that have been less influenced by Western culture. Explore study-abroad programs or consider volunteering with the Peace Corps to get an intense, long-term experience living in another culture.

Visit the Web sites of professional organizations, such as the Society of Ethnobiology and the Botanical Society of America.

## EMPLOYERS

Ethnoscientists work in the same places as other social and life scientists—universities, research institutes, government and non-government organizations, museums, and alternative medical firms. Sometimes ethnoscientists become independent consultants.

Eugene Hunn says, "Most ethnobiologists work at universities as faculty members or researchers. Some may be employed by government agencies, for example, to advise National Park Service or Forest Service staff on issues relating to how local communities, such as Native American groups, interact with local plants and animals. They study how traditional and modern subsistence activities, such as hunting, fishing, gathering, herding, or farming, might affect protected areas. Some ethnoscientists work at museums and herbaria. A few jobs may be available in the private sector, with companies developing new products modeled on how indigenous peoples use plants or animals—for example, drugs, cosmetics, or teas."

## STARTING OUT

While working on your degree, be sure to communicate your interests to your professors. They may be aware of opportunities at the university or elsewhere. You might be able to participate in a university research project or become a research assistant or teaching fellow. Professional organizations are another important resource when it comes to finding a job. If you network with others in your field, you have a good chance of hearing about job opportunities. Also, organizations might post information on jobs, internships, or apprenticeships in their journals or on their Web sites.

There is strong competition for academic positions. Most students begin their job search while finishing their graduate degrees. Your first position is likely to be an instructor in general courses in anthropology, sociology, history, biology, or botany, depending on your specialty. In order to advance to higher ranks of professor, you will be required to do research, during which you can focus on your ethnoscience specialty. Evelyn Mathias suggests that, because research opportunities are difficult to come by, you might have to create your own opportunities, perhaps by proposing research projects.

## ADVANCEMENT

Ethnoscientists advance by producing high-quality research and publishing articles or books. They might come to be known as experts in their field. They might become the head of a research project. The advancement path of ethnoscientists who teach in universities is instructor to assistant professor to associate professor to full professor. A full professor might eventually become a department head.

## EARNINGS

The U.S. Department of Labor reports the mean annual salaries of soil and plant scientists were $59,180 in 2009. Salaries ranged from less than $34,930 to $107,670 or more. Salaries for college-level teachers in the biological sciences ranged from less than $41,060 for the lowest paid 10 percent to more than $155,020 for the highest paid 10 percent during that same year.

Ethnoscientists who work as salaried employees usually receive benefits such as vacation days, sick leave, health and life insurance, and a savings and pension program. Self-employed ethnoscientists must provide their own benefits.

## WORK ENVIRONMENT

Ethnoscientists in academia mainly work indoors. Their time is spent teaching, meeting with students, writing texts or grant proposals, or compiling and analyzing data. Some ethnoscientists cite networking and getting financial support so they can conduct fieldwork as the hardest parts of their jobs. Ethnoscientists who travel to do research on different cultural groups conduct fieldwork outdoors. When in the field, they encounter climates that are different from their own, such as the tropical rainforest or the Arctic tundra. Ethnoscientists must be ready to work outdoors, sometimes for long periods of time, no matter what the weather, and they must be prepared to stay in primitive living conditions.

## OUTLOOK

The *Occupational Outlook Handbook* reports that employment for postsecondary teachers in general will grow faster than the average for all careers through 2018. This is largely because enrollment is expected to increase, creating a greater need for professors. Job growth that is much faster than the average is expected for medical and biological scientists, but scientists holding Ph.D.'s may face strong competition when trying to get basic research positions.

While interest in ethnoscience is growing, the field is still very small, and it is difficult to say whether funding will increase as well. If there are federal budget cuts, there might be a decrease in the amount of money devoted to new government research projects, or existing projects might not get renewed.

## FOR MORE INFORMATION

*For information on careers in anthropology, contact*
**American Anthropological Association**
2200 Wilson Boulevard, Suite 600
Arlington, VA 22201-3357
Tel: 703-528-1902
http://www.aaanet.org

*The AVMA Web site provides information on careers, student chapters, and educational resources.*
**American Veterinary Medical Association (AVMA)**
1931 North Meacham Road, Suite 100
Schaumburg, IL 60173-4360
Tel: 800-248-2862
E-mail: avmainfo@avma.org
http://www.avma.org

*For information on membership, a list of accredited zoos through-
out the world, and careers in aquatic and marine science, including
job listings, contact*
**Association of Zoos and Aquariums**
8403 Colesville Road, Suite 710
Silver Spring, MD 20910-3314
Tel: 301-562-0777
http://www.aza.org

*For information on botany careers, contact*
**Botanical Society of America**
PO Box 299
St. Louis, MO 63166-0299
Tel: 314-577-9566
E-mail: bsa-manager@botany.org
http://www.botany.org

*For information on careers in ecology, contact*
**Ecological Society of America**
1990 M Street, NW, Suite 700
Washington, DC 20036-3415
Tel: 202-833-8773
E-mail: esahq@esa.org
http://www.esa.org

*For more information about ethnopharmacology, visit the society's
Web site.*
**International Society for Ethnopharmacology**
http://www.ethnopharmacology.org

*For more information about ethnobiology, contact*
**International Society of Ethnobiology**
14 School Street
PO Box 303
Bristol, VT 05443-0303
Tel: 802-453-6996
E-mail: isecoordinator@gmail.com
http://www.ethnobiology.net

*This society offers membership to college students and presents its
newsletter online.*
**Society for Economic Botany**
PO Box 299
St. Louis, MO 63166-0299

E-mail: seb@econbot.org
http://www.econbot.org

*This society offers membership to college students.*
**Society of Ethnobiology**
Department of Geography
University of North Texas
1155 Union Circle #305279
Denton, TX 76203-5017
Tel: 940-565-4987
E-mail: secretary@ethnobiology.org
http://ethnobiology.org

# Forensic Biologists

## OVERVIEW

*Biologists* study the origin, development, anatomy, function, distribution, and other basic principles of living organisms. They are concerned with the nature of life itself in humans, microorganisms, plants, and animals, and with the relationship of each organism to its environment. *Forensic biologists* are specialized biologists who employ scientific principles and methods to analyze biological specimens so they can be used as evidence in a court of law.

## HISTORY

Biological materials—such as blood and other bodily fluids, and bones, hair, nails, skin, and other bodily tissues—have been used informally for hundreds, if not thousands of years, to convict or acquit the accused. But forensic biology as we know it today can only be traced back to the 1830s. The first procedures for the microscopic detection of sperm were published in 1839, according to the Forensic Science Timeline (http://www.forensicdna.com/Timeline020702.pdf), a Web site by Norah Rudin and Keith Inman. In 1853, the German histologist Ludwig Teichmann developed a test for the presence of blood.

In the following years, new tests, investigative methods, and scientific equipment were developed, which created a demand for formalized settings where evidence could be studied. In 1910, the first police crime laboratory was founded at the University of Lyons in France. The first forensic laboratory in the United States was founded in 1923 in Los Angeles, California. In 1932, the Federal Bureau of Investigation crime lab was created. Also in the 1930s, biological evidence was used to solve the kidnapping and murder of

### QUICK FACTS

**School Subjects**
Biology
Speech

**Personal Skills**
Technical/scientific

**Work Environment**
Indoors and outdoors
Primarily multiple locations

**Minimum Education Level**
Bachelor's degree

**Salary Range**
$36,750 to $66,510 to
$100,580+

**Certification or Licensing**
Voluntary

**Outlook**
About as fast as the average

**DOT**
041

**GOE**
02.03.03

**NOC**
2121

**O*NET-SOC**
19-1020.01, 19-1029.00

aviator Charles Lindbergh's baby boy. Wood from a homemade ladder left at the crime scene was matched with wood from the home of the individual who was accused of the crime. This was the first time that forensic botanical evidence, a branch of forensics biology, was accepted in an American court.

The field of forensic biology experienced major advances in 1944 when Oswald Avery and a team of scientists were able to isolate and identify DNA as the transmitter of genetic information. In 1953, James Watson, Francis Crick, and Maurice Wilkins deciphered the complex structure of DNA and predicted that it carried the genetic code for all living matter. The first DNA profiling test was developed in 1984, and in 1987 DNA profiling was used for the first time to catch a murderer and exonerate an individual accused of a crime (both during the same investigation). Today, DNA testing has become one of the major tools of forensic biologists, who continue to use this and other methods to help solve crimes.

## THE JOB

Forensic biologists analyze biological materials, such as blood, saliva, and other bodily fluids, bones, hair, nails, skin, and other bodily tissue. They may also work with nonhuman-based biological samples, such as those from plants or animals. It is the responsibility of the forensic biologist to analyze the biological material using various laboratory procedures and document their findings so they can be presented as evidence in legal proceedings.

Some forensic biologists work at crime scenes to identify and collect biological specimens that can be used as evidence, but most forensic biologists primarily work in a laboratory, handling biological material that has already been collected and delivered to them. A forensic biologist employs different methods to study and analyze biological evidence. Biological samples first must be catalogued and photographed, if this has not already been done before they have reached the forensic biologist. The samples may be viewed by high-magnification instruments, such as microscopes, and/or subjected to any number of biological-based tests or procedures. DNA analysis—where DNA genetic markers from biological evidence collected at a crime scene are compared to DNA markers in other samples—is one such method used by forensic biologists. DNA analysis can establish whether any of the biological evidence collected at a crime scene could have come from a suspect in the case at hand, or if it matches any of the entries in CODIS (Combined DNA Index System), the national DNA databank maintained by the Federal Bureau of Investigation. Depending on what type of biological sample is being analyzed and the type of test that is used, forensic biologists can sometimes determine many characteristics useful to a criminal investigation, such as the sex, age, or other descriptors of the person (or animal, as the case may be) from whom the biological sample was obtained.

Because the biological samples being analyzed are primarily intended to be used as evidence in a court of law, forensic biologists must take great care to carefully handle the samples, take detailed notes about how and what was done to them through the course of any tests or procedures, and prepare clear but thorough reports that document their findings. This must be done to ensure that important evidence is allowed to be used for consideration in legal proceedings, rather than being dismissed for such reasons as the fact that a forensic biologist forgot to document part of a test, a sample was not maintained at the proper temperature, or evidence was misplaced due to inappropriate cataloguing procedures. Many forensic biologists testify in court regarding their findings or to explain the science so that people without a background in science can understand the relevance of the biological evidence.

Some forensic biologists routinely work with nonhuman based samples. They might be involved in investigations of animal abuse, outbreaks of disease in a specific animal population, or illegal activity connected to endangered species. They might also be involved in investigating environmental contaminants or threats to public health.

Although most forensic biologists are civilian workers, some are sworn law enforcement officers.

## REQUIREMENTS

### High School
High school students interested in a career in forensic biology should take English, biology, physics, chemistry, Latin, geometry, and algebra.

### Postsecondary Training
You will need a minimum of a bachelor's degree in biology, microbiology, biochemistry, forensic science, chemistry, or a related field to work as a forensic biologist. Prospective forensic biologists should also obtain broad undergraduate college training. In addition to courses in all phases of biology, useful related courses include organic and inorganic chemistry, molecular biology, biochemistry,

physics, and mathematics. Modern languages, English, biometrics (the use of mathematics in biological measurements), and statistics are also useful. Courses in computers will be extremely beneficial. Students should take advantage of courses that require laboratory, field, or collecting work. Important coursework for those who want to specialize in DNA analysis include genetics, molecular biology, statistics, and biochemistry.

Nearly all postsecondary institutions offer undergraduate training in one or more of the biological sciences. These vary from liberal arts schools that offer basic majors in botany and zoology to large universities that permit specialization in areas such as entomology, bacteriology, and physiology at the undergraduate level.

For the highest professional status, a doctorate is required. This is particularly true of top research positions and most higher-level college teaching openings. Many colleges and universities offer courses leading to a master's degree and a doctorate.

The American Academy of Forensic Sciences offers a list of colleges and universities that offer degrees in forensic biology and related fields at its Web site, http://www.aafs.org.

New forensic biologists typically participate in on-the-job training that lasts from six months to two years. They also continue to learn throughout their careers by participating in seminars, workshops, and other educational activities.

## Certification or Licensing

The International Association for Identification offers several certification categories that may be of interest to forensic biologists, including certified crime scene analyst and bloodstain pattern examiner certification. Contact the association for more information.

The American College of Forensic Examiners offers the certified forensic consultant program, which provides an overview of the U.S. judicial system, and would be a good option for forensic biologists who testify in court. Contact the college for more information.

## Other Requirements

Forensic biologists must be systematic in their approach to collecting and analyzing evidence. They should have probing, inquisitive minds and an aptitude for biology, chemistry, and mathematics. Patience and imagination are also required since they may spend much time analyzing evidence and data. Forensic biologists must also have good communication skills in order to effectively gather and exchange data and solve problems that arise in their work. These skills will especially come in handy for those who testify in court.

## EXPLORING

You can measure your aptitude and interest in the work of biologists by taking courses in the field. Laboratory assignments, for example, provide information on techniques used by the working biologist. Many schools hire students as laboratory assistants to work directly under a teacher and help administer the laboratory sections of courses.

School assemblies, field trips to government and private crime laboratories and research centers, and career conferences provide additional insight into career opportunities. Advanced students often are able to attend professional meetings and seminars.

Part-time and summer positions in biology or related areas are particularly helpful. Students with some college courses in biology may find summer positions as laboratory assistants. Graduate students may find work on research projects conducted by their institutions. Beginning college and advanced high school students may find employment as laboratory aides or hospital orderlies or attendants. Despite the menial nature of these positions, they afford a useful insight into careers in biology. High school students often have the opportunity to join volunteer service groups at local hospitals. Student science training programs allow qualified high school students to spend a summer doing research under the supervision of a scientist. They can also participate in biology-related summer experience programs and camps at colleges and universities.

You can also ask your science teacher to arrange an interview with a forensic biologist, read books about the field (such as *Essential Forensic Biology*, by Alan Gunn), surf the Web to learn more about forensic biology, and attend court proceedings that feature testimony by forensic biologists.

## EMPLOYERS

Forensic biologists work at forensic science laboratories at various governmental levels. They also work for law firms and in academia. Biologists who do not specialize in forensic biology are employed by government agencies, pharmaceutical companies, hospitals, biotechnology companies, laboratories, and a wide variety of other employers.

## STARTING OUT

Forensic biologists should apply directly to forensic science laboratories for employment opportunities. Governmental agencies that employ forensic biologists often interview college seniors on campus. Private and public employment offices frequently have listings from these employers. Opportunities may also be found through college career services offices and through contacts made while participating in internships.

Special application procedures are required for positions with government agencies. Civil service applications for federal, state, and municipal positions may be obtained by writing to the agency involved and from high school and college career services offices and public employment agencies.

## ADVANCEMENT

With the right qualifications, the forensic biologist may advance to the position of project chief and direct a team of other forensic biologists. Many use their knowledge and experience as background for administrative and management positions. Often, as they develop professional expertise, forensic biologists move from strictly technical assignments into positions in which they interpret biological knowledge.

Some forensic biologists become technical specialists in a field such as DNA analysis. Others move on to larger agencies or more prestigious cases. Some become college professors or educators at other academic levels.

## EARNINGS

There is no comprehensive salary information available for forensic biologists. The U.S. Department of Labor (DOL) does provide information on biologists, not otherwise classified (a category that includes forensic biologists). The median salary for these professionals was $66,510 in 2009. Salaries ranged from less than $36,750 to $100,580 or more. In 2009 biological scientists working for the federal government earned a mean annual salary of $73,030, and those employed by colleges and universities earned $53,990. Earnings for forensic biologists vary extensively based on the type and size of their employer, the individual's level of education and experience, and other factors.

Forensic biologists are usually eligible for health and dental insurance, paid vacations and sick days, and retirement plans. Some employers may offer reimbursement for continuing education, seminars, and travel.

# WORK ENVIRONMENT

The forensic biologist's work environment varies greatly depending upon the position and type of employer. One forensic biologist may frequently travel to and work at crime scenes and may be required to move bodies or investigative equipment. Another spends most of his or her time working in a laboratory. Many forensic biologists work with toxic substances, human tissues and fluids, and potentially harmful chemicals and disease cultures; strict safety measures must be observed. Some must testify in court and participate in recorded depositions. Courtrooms can sometimes be tense and stressful places, and forensic biologists should be able to defend their findings under sometimes harsh questioning from defense attorneys or other individuals involved in the case.

# OUTLOOK

The DOL predicts that employment for biological scientists will grow much faster than the average for all careers through 2018, although competition will be stiff for some positions. For example, Ph.D.'s looking for research positions will find strong competition for a limited number of openings. In addition, certain government jobs as well as government funding for research may also be less plentiful. A recession or shift in political power can cause the loss of funding for forensic science laboratories. Biologists with advanced degrees will be best qualified for the most lucrative and challenging jobs, although this varies by specialty, with genetic, cellular, and biochemical research showing the most promise. Scientists with bachelor's degrees may find openings as science or engineering technicians or as health technologists and technicians. Many colleges and universities are cutting back on their faculties, but high schools and two-year colleges may have teaching positions available.

Employment opportunities should also be good for those who specialize in forensic biology. There have been major developments in evidence analysis (especially DNA) in the past 25 years, and these new techniques have created demand for forensic biologists. It is important to remember that the field of forensic biology is small, and there is strong competition for jobs in the field. Opportunities should be best for experienced forensic biologists with advanced training in the field.

# FOR MORE INFORMATION

*For information on forensic careers and education, contact*
**American Academy of Forensic Sciences**
410 North 21st Street
Colorado Springs, CO 80904-2712
Tel: 719-636-1100
http://www.aafs.org

*For information on forensic science and certification, contact*
**American College of Forensic Examiners International**
2750 East Sunshine Street
Springfield, MO 65804-2047
Tel: 800-423-9737
http://www.acfei.com

*For information on careers in biology, contact*
**American Institute of Biological Sciences**
1444 I Street, NW, Suite 200
Washington, DC 20005-6535
Tel: 202-628-1500
http://www.aibs.org

*For more information on physiology, contact*
**American Physiological Society**
9650 Rockville Pike
Bethesda, MD 20814-3991
Tel: 301-634-7164
http://www.the-aps.org

*For information on careers, educational resources, and fellowships,*
*contact*
**American Society for Microbiology**
1752 N Street, NW
Washington, DC 20036-2904
Tel: 202-737-3600
http://www.asm.org

*For general information about plant biology, contact*
**American Society of Plant Biologists**
http://www.aspb.org

*For useful forensic science Web links, visit the association's Web site.*
**Association of Forensic DNA Analysts and Administrators**
PO Box 4983
Austin, TX 78765-4983
http://www.afdaa.org

*For career information, including articles and books on the biotechnology industry, contact*
**Biotechnology Industry Organization**
1201 Maryland Avenue, SW, Suite 900
Washington, DC 20024-2149
Tel: 202-962-9200
E-mail: info@bio.org
http://www.bio.org

*To learn more about forensic services at the FBI, visit the FBI Laboratory Division's Web site.*
**Federal Bureau of Investigation (FBI)**
J. Edgar Hoover Building
935 Pennsylvania Avenue, NW
Washington, DC 20535-0001
Tel: 202-324-3000
http://www.fbi.gov/hq/lab/labhome.htm

*For information on certification, contact*
**International Association for Identification**
2535 Pilot Knob Road, Suite 117
Mendota Heights, MN 55120-1120
Tel: 651-681-8566
http://www.theiai.org

*For information about the field, visit the society's Web site.*
**International Society for Forensic Genetics**
http://www.isfg.org

*For information on specific careers in biology (including forensic biology), contact*
**National Institutes of Health**
9000 Rockville Pike
Bethesda, MD 20892-0001
Tel: 301-496-4000
E-mail: NIHinfo@od.nih.gov
http://www.nih.gov

# Genetic Scientists

**School Subjects**
Biology
Chemistry

**Personal Skills**
Communication/ideas
Technical/scientific

**Work Environment**
Primarily indoors
Primarily one location

**Minimum Education Level**
Bachelor's degree

**Salary Range**
$27,431 to $75,000 to
$138,840+

**Certification or Licensing**
Required for certain positions

**Outlook**
Faster than the average

**DOT**
041

**GOE**
02.03.03

**NOC**
2121

**O*NET-SOC**
19-1029.03, 19-1042.00

## OVERVIEW

*Genetic scientists*, or *geneticists*, study heredity. They study plants as well as animals, including humans. Geneticists conduct research on how characteristics are passed from one generation to the next through the genes present in each cell of an organism. This research often involves manipulating or altering particular genetic characteristics to better understand how genetic systems work. For instance, genetic scientists may breed a family of mice with a tendency toward high blood pressure to test the effects of exercise or diet on that condition. Their work adds to the body of biological knowledge and helps prevent inheritable diseases. Genetics is a component of just about every area of biology and can be found in many biology subfields. Rapidly growing specialty areas include the fields of genetic counseling and medical genetics, and genomic medicine (the use of genetic information to improve health outcomes).

## HISTORY

In the 1860s, an Austrian monk named Gregor Mendel discovered the principles of genetics by breeding different varieties of garden peas in his monastery garden. His experiments, which showed that crossing short and tall peas produced only tall plants rather than any of medium height, proved that no blending of traits occurred. Rather, tallness was the dominant (or more powerful) trait and shortness was recessive.

Fifty years after Mendel's discoveries, American biologist Thomas Hunt Morgan discovered that genes are located on the chromosomes present in every cell. Genes are like a blueprint; they carry instructions for how an organism—human, animal, or plant—will be built. However, as Hugo de Vries discovered in his research in the early 1900s, genes do not always copy themselves exactly. Sometimes they mutate, that is, change their blueprint from one generation to the next. Mutations are often responsible for illness.

The modern history of genetics began in the early 1950s with James Watson's and Francis Crick's discovery of the double helix, or spiral ladder, structure of DNA. Their discovery touched off a flurry of scientific activity that led to a better understanding of DNA chemistry and the genetic code. Before 1975, however, the technology for actually altering the genes of organisms for study or practical use was severely limited. For while the 1950s and 1960s saw big successes in gene transfer and molecular biology for the smaller and simpler bacteria cells, more complex organisms were another story. Even though both plant and animal cells could be grown in culture, the detailed workings of their genes remained a mystery until the discovery of recombinant DNA techniques. Recombinant DNA refers to combining the DNA, or genetic material, from two separate organisms to form unique DNA molecules that carry a new combination of genes. The major tools of this technology—and the second most important discovery in the field of genetics—are restriction enzymes, first discovered in the 1960s. They work by cutting up DNA molecules at particular points so that DNA pieces from different sources may be joined. These genetically engineered cells may then be cloned, or grown in culture, to make copies of the desired gene. The cloning of genetically engineered cells has many potentially useful applications for society, such as producing pest-resistant plants, altering bacteria for waste cleanup, or generating proteins for medical uses like dissolving blood clots or making human growth hormone.

The most ambitious project in DNA research to date made possible by advanced technology was the effort to map the entire human genome, or all the genetic material in human beings. Called the Human Genome Project (HGP), it is considered more important to science history than either the splitting of the atom or the moon landing. The U.S. government launched the HGP in 1990, with the goal of completing the sequencing by 2005. In 1998, Celera Genomics Corporation (a for-profit company) announced that it would start its own sequencing project to compete with the HGP. By 2000 (four years ahead of schedule), both organizations had completed rough drafts of the human genome. Project results promise new scientific knowledge, medicines, and therapies that can be used to battle diseases such as AIDS, cancer, arthritis, and osteoporosis. Continuing advances in automation and electronics, including use of the latest computer software, will greatly promote project goals and increase our understanding of genetics.

## THE JOB

The goal of genetic scientists is to increase knowledge in order to do a variety of things, such as understand, and treat disease; decrease the risk for morbidity and mortality (illness and death) from genetic disease; counsel families at risk of having children with genetic disorders; and breed new crops and livestock, among other things. These goals can be obtained in a laboratory or clinical setting. Many geneticists spend their time in a laboratory isolating particular genes in tissue samples and doing experiments to find out which characteristics those genes are responsible for. They work with chemicals, heat, light, and such instruments as microscopes, computers, electron microscopes, and other technical equipment. Besides having excellent mathematical and analytical skills, which will help them design and carry out experiments and analyze results, genetic scientists must also develop good writing and teaching techniques. They must be able to communicate their research results to students in classroom settings and to colleagues through published papers. Other geneticists see patients in a clinical setting. Patients with physical changes or developmental concerns may be seen by a *clinical geneticist* or *genetic counselor*. Clinical geneticists will provide patients with a physical examination, looking for subtle differences that may indicate a specific genetic condition. Genetic counselors discuss the results of the physical exam, genetic testing options and the implications of the genetic testing and condition to the individual and family. Genetic testing, performed by the laboratory geneticists, can provide answers to physical or developmental concerns that are identified by the clinical geneticists.

Profound academic and technological advances made over the last two decades have brought about rapid progress in the field. Some of the many specialty areas for genetic scientists are described here.

*Research geneticists* typically complete a Ph.D. program, carrying out original research under a faculty member's direction. After earning their Ph.D.'s, most graduates do research for two to four years as postdoctoral fellows. Following this training, they are then qualified to hold faculty positions at academic institutions or to join the staffs of research institutes or biotechnology firms.

*Laboratory geneticists* apply modern genetic technology to agriculture, police work, pharmaceutical development, and clinical medicine. They typically have four to six years of college and are part of a staff of scientists trained in molecular biology, cytogenetics, biochemical genetics, immunogenetics, and related disciplines. Some genetic laboratories require their staff members to have specific training and certification in cytogenetic or medical technology.

As mentioned earlier, some geneticists specialize as genetic counselors. Genetic counselors are health professionals with a master's degree specializing in medical genetics and counseling. They work as a valuable part of a health care team, giving information and support to families affected by birth defects or genetic disorders, individuals who themselves have genetic conditions and couples concerned about having a child with a genetic condition. Genetic counselors identify family members who are at risk for disease by generating family medical histories and obtaining and interpreting information about genetic conditions. They discuss how genetic testing can detect possible gene changes and the likelihood of a genetic disease occurring in other family members, including children. Genetic counselors go through available options with their patients, serving as patient advocates and making referrals to community or state support services. Some genetic counselors serve in administrative roles, while others conduct research activities related to the field of medical genetics and genetic counseling.

Clinical geneticists are generally medical doctors, having received an M.D. degree and completed a pediatric, internal medicine, family medicine or obstetric residency, followed by a genetics fellowship or residency. Many clinical geneticists work at university medical centers or large hospitals, while some have private practices or work in biotechnology companies. Generally, this job involves recognizing genetic disorders and birth defects in patients, arranging the proper medical management, and helping the patient and family understand and cope with the diagnosis. Some clinical geneticists work primarily with infants and children, while others may specialize in the genetic problems of babies still in the womb. They may also work with adult patients with inherited forms of heart disease, cancer, or neurological disease. An important role for the clinical geneticist is being the link between the research geneticists who are constantly advancing the field and the patients who stand to benefit from their discoveries.

*Cytogenetic technologists* prepare, analyze and examine chromosome structure. Living cells are first treated with a special stain that reveals stripes of light and dark regions along the length of each chromosome. Because the stripes are highly specific for a particular chromosome, stripe patterns help differentiate chromosomes from one another, making any abnormalities in structure easily seen. Chromosome analysis may be performed on just about any living tissue, but for clinical work, it usually is done on amniotic fluid (fluid surrounding the fetus), chorionic villi (fetal placenta), blood, saliva samples, buccal smears (cells from the inside of the cheek), bone marrow, and miscarriages.

*Molecular geneticists* study and analyze cellular DNA to identify genetic abnormalities. The majority of their work focuses on three areas: prenatal diagnosis (examining fetal cells for possible abnormalities), carrier testing (examining cells to determine if an individual is at risk from a single gene disorder), and confirmation of diagnosis (testing samples provided by other health care professionals to confirm or contradict a diagnosis).

An offshoot of cytogenetics, *forensic genetics*, is used by the law enforcement community to perform DNA fingerprinting, a subspecialty that is currently booming. Alec Jeffreys, a professor at Leicester University, discovered that each of us has highly specific patterns within our DNA located on many different chromosomes. The pattern is so distinctive that no two people's DNA are the same, except for identical twins, which is why the technique is called DNA fingerprinting. It has been used to identify and convict criminals and to determine parentage.

*Genetic engineers* experiment with altering, splicing, and rearranging genes for specific results. This research has resulted in the discovery and production of insulin and interferon, two medical breakthroughs that can treat diseases like diabetes and leukemia. Genetic engineering successes have also been seen in agricultural science. Agricultural triumphs like hybrid corn, disease-resistant grains, and higher-quality livestock are all products of the principles of recombinant DNA and cloning.

Another specialty area for geneticists is population genetics. *Population geneticists* look at allele frequency within populations and how they change during immigration, emigration and through evolution. They can look at mutations that occur spontaneously or are introduced purposely in farm animals and crops, to produce a marketable result.

## REQUIREMENTS

### High School

If you are interested in becoming a geneticist working in basic research, you should study math, chemistry, and physics in high school, along with biology. English, writing, and computer studies are helpful for developing communications skills. A college degree is a must.

## Postsecondary Training

In college, students wishing to become genetic scientists typically major in biology or genetics, taking math, chemistry, and physics courses. However, you could also major in any one of the physical sciences with a minor in biology and still enter graduate school in the field of genetics. Laboratory geneticists, including molecular geneticists, cytogeneticists, biochemical geneticists, and others require a doctoral degree and post-doctorate training. Clinical geneticists usually earn an M.D. degree, which requires getting admitted to medical school, then completing a three- to-five-year residency in a medical specialty followed by an additional two to three years of specialized training in genetics.

Career opportunities also exist for those with bachelor's or master's of science degrees, particularly in the rapidly growing biotechnology field, which is using genetics to produce everything from medicines to microchips. This industry needs well-trained research technicians who typically have a bachelor of science degree in biology with a molecular or biochemistry emphasis. The federal government also has a need for research technicians and hires college graduates and those with master's degrees to work in hospitals and U.S. Department of Agriculture (USDA) laboratories. Cytogenetic technologists generally need a bachelor of science degree.

Genetic counselors usually hold master's degrees. Training programs for genetic counselors are two-year master's-level programs with courses and field training in medical genetics and counseling.

## Certification or Licensing

Licensing and/or certification may be necessary, depending on the specialty that is chosen. Molecular geneticists, cytogeneticists, biochemical geneticists, and clinical geneticists may obtain certification through the American Board of Medical Genetics (http://www.abmg.org) while genetic counselors are certified by the American Board of Genetic Counseling (http://www.abgc.net). Additionally, clinical geneticists must be licensed to practice medicine, and some states now require genetic counselors to obtain a license. Some genetic laboratories require staff to have specific training and certification in cytogenetic or medical technology, while others hire people with relevant B.S. or M.S. degrees as long as they show an aptitude for the work.

### Other Requirements

Geneticists must be smart and have inquiring minds. They need to be able to evaluate results and draw conclusions from measurable criteria. They should also be able to work with abstract theories and ideas, and in cooperation with others. Both written and verbal communications skills are important for sharing research information. Important personal qualities for laboratory scientists are patience, attention to detail, and determination. Genetic counselors must have mature judgment and strong communications skills to deal with people coping with highly emotional issues. They must be able to establish trust quickly and have the right mix of objectivity (the ability to be neutral) and sensitivity to do their work well.

## EXPLORING

As a high school student, you can prepare for a career as a genetic scientist by taking as many courses in math and science as you can. You should also develop your writing and computer skills. High school science teachers can often contact departments of biology and genetics at nearby colleges and universities and arrange field trips or college speakers. Speakers can give you information about university summer programs. Take advantage of these and other opportunities offered in your community through community colleges, museums, professional associations, and special interest groups.

## EMPLOYERS

Genetic scientists work for a variety of employers, including biotechnology firms, research centers, government agencies, colleges, universities, medical centers, and agricultural stations and farms. The USDA, the Fish and Wildlife Service, the National Institutes of Health, and several other government agencies have laboratories that employ genetic scientists.

## STARTING OUT

Because this career is so broad with many varied fields within it, methods of entry also vary, depending on the specialty area you choose. As early as high school, opportunities exist for paid and unpaid internships at a number of science laboratories. Job seekers can get leads from their professors or fellow students. You could join a team of researchers as a laboratory aide or technician.

Federal agencies often come to college campuses to recruit graduates. If you are interested in a job with the federal government, visit http://www.fedjobs.gov for more information. Federal agencies also come to college campuses to recruit graduates.

If you would like to work at a college or university after completing an advanced degree, you may wish to continue your education through a postdoctoral fellowship, assisting a prominent scientist with research. Joining a professional organization, such as the American Society of Human Genetics, the American College of Medical Genetics, or the National Society of Genetic Counselors can also provide you with the network to find open positions. Colleges and universities advertise open positions in professional journals and in the *Chronicle of Higher Education* (http://chronicle.com), available at public libraries. You should also consult pharmaceutical and biotechnology companies' departments of human resources for employment opportunities in those industries.

## ADVANCEMENT

At colleges and universities, beginning teachers and researchers are hired at the assistant professor level. With additional years of experience and an impressive level of published research and teaching, they are promoted to associate professor and then to full professor. Many times, individuals go through the process to obtain tenure. Similar years of experience lead to promotion in private industry and government agencies. Promotion usually involves an increase in salary as well as more job duties and greater work prominence.

## EARNINGS

Genetic scientists with a bachelor's degree hired by the federal government at the GS-5 entry level earned average starting salaries of $27,431 in 2010. For those with a master's degree, who qualified to start at the GS-7 or GS-9 levels, the beginning salary was $33,979 and $41,563, respectively. Doctoral degree holders who qualified to start at the GS-11 level earned $50,287. Experienced geneticists employed by the federal government earned average salaries of $99,752 in 2009. The average salary for genetic scientists working in private industry is approximately $75,000, with biotechnology firms offering even higher salaries. Salaries for all medical scientists ranged from less than $41,320 to $138,840 or more in 2009.

In 2009, the median salary for genetic counselors was $58,184, according to a professional status survey by the National Society of

Genetic Counselors. Salaries for the middle 50 percent ranged from $54,305 to $65,011.

Benefits for genetic scientists depend on the employer; however, they usually include such items as health insurance, retirement or 401(k) plans, and paid sick and vacation days.

## WORK ENVIRONMENT

Geneticists spend time in laboratories, designing and conducting research experiments. While most of these experiments will take many hours and yield few publishable results, they can result in patents and significant royalties, with the goal of reducing the morbity and mortality from genetic disease. Even small discoveries in the genetics field add to biological knowledge and can lead to disease treatments. Genetic scientists also spend considerable time writing reports about their experiments, lecturing or teaching about their research, and preparing grant proposals to federal or private agencies to secure funding to support their research. Because federal grants are extremely competitive, only the best-written and most scientifically up-to-date proposals will receive funding. Therefore, genetic scientists must keep improving their skills and knowledge throughout their careers to keep up with new developments in the field and to advance their own research. Usually, geneticists work as part of a research team, consisting of graduate students and laboratory personnel, which cooperate on various aspects of their experiments. They may work from nine to five, although they may be required to work late into the night and on weekends during critical periods of an experiment. They may also work extra hours to complete research projects, to write reports of findings, or to read the latest developments in their specialty.

## OUTLOOK

The U.S. Department of Labor predicts that employment for medical scientists will grow much faster than the average for all occupations through 2018. Interest in genetic research has exploded in the past decade, with breakthrough discoveries bringing greater attention to the exciting possibilities of decreasing morbidity and mortality of genetic disease.

Working in an age with virtually no limits, geneticists have the luxury of choosing their focus according to what interests them most. Rapid progress in the field, along with new methods of mapping genetic traits, has put all natural variation in all organisms within the grasp of genetic investigators. It is estimated that every human disease that is caused by a single gene defect will be curable by genetic intervention during the lifetime of students currently in high school. As the need to understand human and animal biology and genetics and the fight to eradicate disease continue, demand for scientists will continue to increase. The world of criminal investigation is increasingly using genetics to win cases, drawing on genetic test results to identify culprits from a drop of blood. Genetics is also being used in food testing to detect contamination by disease-causing organisms.

## FOR MORE INFORMATION

*Visit the board's Web site for information on certification, an overview of the career of genetic counselor, and a list of accredited graduate schools.*

**American Board of Genetic Counseling**
PO Box 14216
Lenexa, KS 66285-4216
Tel: 913-895-4617
E-mail: info@abgc.net
http://www.abgc.net

*Contact the board for information on training and certification for medical geneticists.*

**American Board of Medical Genetics**
9650 Rockville Pike
Bethesda, MD 20814-3998
Tel: 301-634-7315
E-mail: abmg@abmg.org
http://www.abmg.org

*Visit the society's Web site for information on educational programs, membership for college students, and for the guide* Careers in Human Genetics.

**American Society of Human Genetics**
9650 Rockville Pike
Bethesda, MD 20814-3998
Tel: 301-634-7300
http://www.ashg.org

*The goal of the association is to "promote the scientific study of the interrelationship of genetic mechanisms and behavior, both human and animal." Visit its Web site for information on membership for college students.*

Behavior Genetics Association
http://www.bga.org

*Visit the society's Web site for information on publications and membership for graduate students, as well as to read* Careers in Genetics.

Genetics Society of America
9650 Rockville Pike
Bethesda, MD 20814-3999
Tel: 301-634-7300
http://www.genetics-gsa.org

*Visit the society's Web site for comprehensive information on genetic counseling, including career information, a list of postsecondary training programs, and details on membership for college students.*

National Society of Genetic Counselors
401 North Michigan Avenue, 22nd Floor
Chicago, IL 60611-4255
Tel: 312-321-6834
E-mail: nsgc@nsgc.org
http://www.nsgc.org

## INTERVIEW

*W. Andrew Faucett is an assistant professor and director of the Genomics & Public Health Program in the Department of Human Genetics at the Emory University School of Medicine in Atlanta, Georgia. He discussed his career with the editors of* Careers in Focus: Biology.

**Q. What made you want to enter this career?**

**A.** I always found learning new scientific information exciting and easy, and genetics was one of my favorite subjects. Sharing my science knowledge with others was something I enjoyed doing. I spent a few years teaching and working with troubled adolescents in a therapeutic setting and found I liked helping people with problems and helping them make decisions. When I first read about genetic counseling I realized that it would allow me to do both. I considered becoming a physician but really wanted the opportunity and time to talk with patients, rather than the very short patient interactions that are part of routine medicine.

**Q. What is one thing that young people may not know about a career in genetics?**

**A.** Genetics is changing how we practice health care, and a career in genetics will allow you to be involved in those changes. Just the time that you think you understand genetics we learn something new. Genetics will never get stale. Genetic counseling? Use of genetic information will involve complex personal and societal questions and genetic counselors can play a critical role in helping individuals and our society decide how best to use this information.

**Q. Can you tell us about the Genomics & Public Health Program?**

**A.** Currently the program is involved with three major activities and several smaller projects. First we coordinate the Collaboration, Education and Test Translation Program (http://rare diseases.info.nih.gov/cettprogram/default.aspx) for the National Institutes of Health Office of Rare Diseases Research. This program helps make genetic tests available. Second, we work to identify barriers to early detection and testing for boys with Duchenne muscular dystrophy. New treatments are in clinical trials and early identification is becoming even more important. Third, we work with the Centers for Disease Control and Dartmouth College on an educational tool for health care providers on genetics and genetic testing (http://www.iml.dartmouth.edu/education/cme/Genetics). I also have a small project to determine the types of genetic education needed by religious leaders; a project to look at how parents respond to false-positive newborn screening results; teach genetics to physician assistants; and am developing a new genetic counseling training program.

**Q. Can you describe a day in your life on the job?**

**A.** For the first 10 years of my career as a practicing genetic counselor I worked with five to six patients or families per day. Now working in public health genetics on average I spend two hours per day on conference calls and another hour or so in meetings. I usually travel two days per week to attend national and international meetings. My work is split between research, education, and helping to develop new policies. For research I often interview health care providers and laboratory directors. For education I interact with health care providers nationally and medical and physician assistant students on campus. Policy work may involve travel or a local meeting to decide how the Centers for Disease Control should evaluate genetic testing.

**Q. What are the most important personal and professional qualities for people in your career?**

**A.** To be a success as a genetic counselor you need to have a good understanding of science and you need to be able to simplify complex concepts. For the educational and policy work you need to be able to network and build working relationships with health care providers, educators, government employees, and patient advocates. You need to have good listening skills, especially for the secondary messages. I use my counseling skills as much in my policy work as I did when working with patients and families.

**Q. What advice would you give to young people who are interested in the field?**

**A.** Find time to meet with a genetic counselor and someone working in public health. Try explaining those difficult science concepts you learned in class to a friend without any science training. Or try to explain them to a student in middle school. Try helping people make difficult decisions without giving your opinion or trying to steer them in a particular direction. If you can do these things and enjoy doing them, this may be the career for you.

**Q. What is the future employment outlook for genetic scientists?**

**A.** We are just beginning to understand the human genome and just beginning to integrate the information into health care and society. This means there will be lots of jobs and career opportunities in genetics in the future. Currently most genetic counselors have a job before they graduate. There may not be a job in every city, but if you are flexible where you live, it should be easy to find a job in the future in genetics.

# Marine Biologists

## OVERVIEW

*Marine biologists* study species of plants and animals living in saltwater, their interactions with one another, and how they influence and are influenced by environmental factors. Marine biology is a branch of the biological sciences, and biologists in this area work in myriad industries, including government agencies, universities, aquariums, and fish hatcheries, to name a few. They generally work either in a laboratory setting or in the field, which in this case means being in or on the ocean or its margins.

## HISTORY

Marine biologists started to make their study into a real science around the 19th century with a series of British expeditions. In 1872, the HMS *Challenger* set sail with scientists Sir Charles Wyville Thomson and Sir John Murray on the most important oceanographic mission of all time. Over four years, they traveled 69,000 miles and cataloged 4,717 new species of marine plants and animals. Many marine scientists view the reports from this expedition as the basis of modern oceanography.

Before this time, marine scientists believed that sea creatures inhabited only shallow waters. They believed that the intense cold, pressure, and darkness below about 1,800 feet could not support life. Then, in the late 1860s, the HMS *Lightning* and the HMS *Porcupine* made hauls from below 14,400 feet that contained bizarre new creatures.

Scientists began to build precision equipment for measuring oceanic conditions. Among these were thermometers that could gauge the temperature at any depth, containers that could be

## Books to Read

Dinwiddie, Robert, Louise Thomas, and Fabien Cousteau. *Ocean.* Reprint ed. New York: DK Publishing, 2008.

Gerdes, Louise I. *Endangered Oceans.* Farmington Hills, Mich.: Greenhaven Press, 2009.

Kaplan, Eugene H. *Sensuous Seas: Tales of a Marine Biologist.* Princeton, N.J.: Princeton University Press, 2006.

Kurtz, Jeff, and David E. Boruchowitz. *The Simple Guide to Marine Aquariums.* 2d ed. Mail Neptune, N.J.: TFH Publications, 2009.

Lear, Linda J. *Rachel Carson: Witness for Nature.* Boston, Mass.: Mariner Books, 2009.

Mills, Dick. *101 Essential Tips: Aquarium Fish.* New York: DK Adult, 2004.

Norse, Elliott A., and Larry B. Crowder. (eds.) *Marine Conservation Biology: The Science of Maintaining the Sea's Biodiversity.* Washington, D.C.: Island Press, 2005.

Perrin, William F., Bernd Würsig, and J.G.M Thewissen. (eds.) *Encyclopedia of Marine Mammals.* 2d ed. Maryland Heights, Mo.: Academic Press, 2008.

Stephens, Lester D., and Dale R. Calder. *Seafaring Scientist: Alfred Goldsborough Mayor, Pioneer in Marine Biology.* Columbia, S.C.: University of South Carolina Press, 2006.

Tullock, John H. *Water Chemistry for the Marine Aquarium.* Happauge, N.Y.: Barron's Educational Series, 2005.

closed at a desired depth to collect seawater, and coring instruments used to sample bottom sediments. Scientists also figured out techniques for measuring levels of salt, oxygen, and nutrients right on board ship.

Modern innovations such as underwater cameras, oxygen tanks, submersible craft, and heavy-duty diving gear that can withstand extremes of cold and pressure have made it possible for marine biologists to observe sea creatures in their natural habitats.

## THE JOB

Marine biologists study and work with sea creatures in their natural environment, the oceans of the world and tidal pools along shorelines, as well as in laboratories. These scientists are interested in knowing how the ocean's changing conditions, such as temperature and chemical pollutants, can affect the plants and animals that live there. For example, what happens when certain species become extinct or are no longer safe to be eaten? Marine biologists can begin to understand how the world's food supply is diminished and help come up with solutions that can change such problem situations.

The work of these scientists is also important for improving and controlling sport and commercial fishing. Through underwater exploration, marine biologists have discovered that humans are damaging the world's coral reefs. They have also charted the migration of whales and counted the decreasing numbers of certain species. They have observed dolphins being accidentally caught in tuna fishermen's nets. By writing reports and research papers about such discoveries, a marine biologist can inform others about problems that need attention and begin to make important changes that could help the world.

To study plants and animals, marine biologists spend some of their work time in the ocean wearing wetsuits to keep warm (because of the frigid temperature below the surface of the sea) and scuba gear to breathe underwater. They gather specimens with a slurp gun, which sucks fish into a specimen bag without injuring them. They must learn how to conduct their research without damaging the marine environment, which is delicate. Marine biologists must also face the threat to their own safety from dangerous fish and underwater conditions.

Marine biologists also study life in tidal pools along the shoreline. They might collect specimens at the same time of day for days at a time. They would keep samples from different pools separate and keep records of the pool's location and the types and measurements of the specimens taken. This ensures that the studies are as accurate as possible. After collecting specimens, they keep them in a portable aquarium tank onboard ship. After returning to land, which may not be for weeks or months, marine biologists study specimens in a laboratory, often with other scientists working on the same study. They might, for example, check the amount of oxygen in a sea turtle's bloodstream to learn how the turtles can stay underwater for so long, or measure elements in the blood of an arctic fish to discover how it can survive frigid temperatures.

One growing subspecialty is marine biotechnology. *Marine biotechnologists* study ocean organisms that may be used for biotechnological applications, such as drug development or nontoxic coatings that repel fouling organisms such as zebra mussels on intake pipes in power plants.

A marine biologist (*right*) with the National Marine Fisheries Service talks with local residents about a beluga whale that washed ashore near Anchorage, Alaska. The biologist took tissue samples and measurements of the whale to determine the cause of death. *(Al Grillo, AP Photo)*

# REQUIREMENTS

## High School

If you are interested in this career, begin your preparations by taking plenty of high school science classes, such as biology, chemistry, and earth science. Also take math classes and computer science classes, both of which will give you skills that you will use in doing research. In addition, take English classes, which will also help you develop research skills as well as writing skills. And, because you will probably need to extend your education beyond the level of a bachelor's degree, consider taking a foreign language. Many graduate programs require their students to meet a foreign language requirement.

## Postsecondary Training

In college, take basic science courses such as biology, botany, and chemistry. However, your class choices don't end there. For instance, in biology you might be required to choose from marine invertebrate biology, ecology, oceanography, genetics, animal physiology, plant physiology, and aquatic plant biology. You might also be required to choose several more specific classes from such choices as ichthyology, vertebrate structure, population biology, developmental biology, biology of microorganisms, evolution, and cell biology. Classes in other subjects will also be required, such as computer science, math (including algebra, trigonometry, calculus, analytical geometry, and statistics), and physics.

Although it is possible to get a job as a marine biologist with just a bachelor's degree, such jobs likely will be low-paying technician positions with little advancement opportunities. Some positions in the field are available with a master's degree, but most marine biologists have a doctoral degree. Students at the graduate level begin to develop an area of specialization, such as *aquatic chemical ecology* (the study of chemicals and their effect on aquatic environments) and *bioinformatics* (the use of computer science, math, and statistics to analyze genetic information). Master's degree programs generally take two to three years to complete. Programs leading to a Ph.D. typically take four to five years to complete.

## Certification or Licensing

If you are going to be diving, organizations like PADI provide basic certification. Training for scientific diving is more in-depth and

requires passing an exam. It is also critical that divers learn cardio-
pulmonary resuscitation (CPR) and first aid. Also, if you'll be handling hazardous materials such as formaldehyde, strong acids, or
radioactive nucleotides, you must be licensed.

### Other Requirements

You should have an ability to ask questions and solve problems,
observe small details carefully, do research, and analyze mathematical information. You should be inquisitive and must be able to think
for yourself. This is essential to the scientific method. You must use
your creative ability and be inventive in order to design experiments;
these are the scientist's means of asking questions about the natural
world. Working in the field often requires some strength and physical endurance, particularly if you are scuba diving or if you are doing
fieldwork in tidepools, which can involve hiking over miles of shore
at low tide, keeping your footing on slippery rocks, and lifting and
turning stones to find specimens.

## EXPLORING

Explore this career and your interest in it by joining your high
school's science club. If the club is involved in any type of projects
or experiments, you will have the opportunity to begin learning to
work with others on a team as well as develop your science and lab
skills. If you are lucky enough to live in a city with an aquarium,
be sure to get either paid or volunteer work there. This is an excellent way to learn about marine life and about the life of a marine
biologist. Visit the Sea Grant Marine Careers Web site (http://www
.marinecareers.net) for links to information on internships, volunteerships, and other activities, such as sea camps.

   You can begin diving training while you are in high school. If you
are between the ages of 10 and 14, you can earn a junior open water
diver certification from PADI. When you turn 15 you can upgrade
your certification to open water diver.

## EMPLOYERS

Employers in this field range from pharmaceutical companies
researching marine sources for medicines to federal agencies that
regulate marine fisheries, such as the National Oceanic and Atmospheric Administration's National Marine Fisheries Service. Aquariums hire marine biologists to collect and study specimens.

After acquiring many years of experience, marine biologists with Ph.D.'s may be eligible for faculty positions at academic and research institutions such as the Scripps Institution of Oceanography or the University of Washington's School of Oceanography.

Marine products companies that manufacture carrageenan and agar (extracted from algae and used as thickening agents in foods) hire marine biologists to design and carry out research.

Jobs in marine biology are based mostly in coastal areas, though some biologists work inland as university professors or perhaps as *marine paleontologists* who search for and study marine fossils.

## STARTING OUT

With a bachelor's degree only, you may be able to get a job as a laboratory technician in a state or federal agency. Some aquaria will hire you straight out of college, but generally it's easier to get a paid position if you have worked as a volunteer at an aquarium. You will need a more advanced degree to get into more technical positions such as consulting, writing for scientific journals, and conducting research.

Web sites are good resources for employment information. If you can find the human resources section of an aquarium's home page, it will tell you whom to contact to find out about openings and may even provide job listings. Federal agencies may also have Web sites with human resource information.

Professors who know you as a student might be able to help you locate a position through their contacts in the professional world.

Another good way to make contacts is by attending conferences or seminars sponsored by aquatic science organizations such as the American Society of Limnology and Oceanography or the Mid-Atlantic Marine Education Association.

## ADVANCEMENT

Lab technicians with four-year degrees may advance to become senior lab techs after years with the same lab. Generally, though, taking on greater responsibility or getting into more technical work means having more education. Those wanting to do research (in any setting) will need a graduate degree or at least be working on one. To get an administrative position with a marine products company or a faculty position at a university, marine biologists need at least a master's degree, and those wanting to become senior scientists at a marine station or full professors must have a doctoral degree.

## EARNINGS

Salaries vary quite a lot depending on factors such as the person's level of education, the type of work (research, teaching, etc.), the size, location, and type of employer (for example, large university, government agency, or private company), and the person's level of work experience. According to the National Association of Colleges and Employers, those seeking their first job and holding bachelor's degrees in biological and life sciences had average salary offers of $33,254 in July 2009. The American Society of Limnology and Oceanography reports that those with bachelor's degrees may start out working for federal government agencies at the pay grades GS-5 to GS-7. In 2010 the yearly earnings at the GS-5 level ranged from $27,431 to $35,657, and yearly earnings at the GS-7 level ranged from $33,979 to $44,176. College biological science teachers (including those who specialize in marine biology) had median annual salaries of $73,980 in 2009, according to the U.S. Department of Labor. Salaries ranged from less than $41,060 to more than $155,020. Marine biologists who hold top-ranking positions and have much experience, such as senior research scientists, may make more than these amounts.

Benefits vary by employer but often include such extras as health insurance and retirement plans.

## WORK ENVIRONMENT

Most marine biologists don't actually spend a lot of time diving. However, researchers might spend a couple of hours periodically breathing from a scuba tank below some waters, like Monterey Bay or the Gulf of Maine. They might gather samples from the deck of a large research vessel during a two-month expedition, or they might meet with several other research biologists.

In most marine biology work, some portion of time is spent in the lab, analyzing samples of seawater or collating data on a computer. Many hours are spent in solitude, reading papers in scientific journals or writing papers for publication.

Instructors or professors work in classrooms interacting with students and directing student lab work.

Those who work for an aquarium, as consultants for private corporations, or in universities work an average of 40 to 50 hours a week.

## OUTLOOK

There are more marine biologists than there are top positions at present. Changes in the earth's environment, such as global climate change and increased levels of heavy metals in the global water cycle, will most likely prompt more research and result in slightly more jobs in different subfields. Education is extremely important in this field. Most marine biologists in basic research positions have a Ph.D. Those with just a bachelor's or master's degree often work as science or engineering technicians, high school biology teachers, and in nonscientist positions related to biology such as marketing, sales, publishing, and research management.

Greater need for smart management of the world's fisheries, research by pharmaceutical companies into deriving medicines from marine organisms, and cultivation of marine food alternatives such as seaweeds and plankton are other factors that may increase the demand for marine biologists in the near future. Because of strong competition for jobs, however, employment should grow about as fast as the average for all careers.

## FOR MORE INFORMATION

*For information on fisheries science, contact*
**American Fisheries Society**
5410 Grosvenor Lane
Bethesda, MD 20814-2144
Tel: 301-897-8616
http://www.fisheries.org

*The Education section of the institute's Web site has information on a number of careers in biology.*
**American Institute of Biological Sciences**
1444 I Street, NW, Suite 200
Washington, DC 20005-6535
Tel: 202-628-1500
http://www.aibs.org

*For information on careers, education, and publications, contact*
**American Society of Limnology and Oceanography**
5400 Bosque Boulevard, Suite 680
Waco, TX 76710-4459
Tel: 800-929-2756
E-mail: business@aslo.org
http://www.aslo.org

*Contact the society for ocean news and information on membership.*
**The Oceanography Society**
PO Box 1931
Rockville, MD 20849-1931
Tel: 301-251-7708
E-mail: info@tos.org
http://www.tos.org

*For information on diving instruction and certification, contact*
**PADI**
30151 Tomas Street
Rancho Santa Margarita, CA 92688-2125
Tel: 800-729-7234
http://www.padi.com

*This center for research and education in global science currently runs more than 300 research programs and uses a fleet of four ships to conduct expeditions over the entire globe. For more information, contact*
**Scripps Institution of Oceanography**
University of California–San Diego
8602 La Jolla Shores Drive
La Jolla, CA 92037-1508
Tel: 858-534-3624
E-mail: scrippsnews@ucsd.edu
http://www-sio.ucsd.edu

*For links to career information and sea programs, visit the following Web sites:*
**Careers in Oceanography, Marine Science, and Marine Biology**
http://ocean.peterbrueggeman.com/career.html

**Sea Grant Marine Careers**
http://www.marinecareers.net

*For reference lists, links to marine labs, summer intern and course opportunities, and links to career information, check out the following Web site:*
**Marine Biology Web**
http://life.bio.sunysb.edu/marinebio/mbweb.html

# Microbiologists

## OVERVIEW

*Microbiologists* are scientists who study living things that cannot be seen with the naked eye, such as bacteria, fungi, protozoans, and viruses, as well as human and animal cells. They examine the effects these microorganisms and infectious agents have on people, animals, plants, and the environment. They are interested in learning about microorganisms that cause diseases, how microorganisms can be used to treat and prevent diseases, and ways microorganisms can be used in developing products. There are approximately 16,900 microbiologists employed in the United States.

## HISTORY

Microbiology traces its beginnings back to the invention of the microscope. Father and son Dutch spectacle makers Hans and Zacharias Jansen are credited with inventing the first actual functioning compound microscope in the 1590s. Another early and important event occurred when Dutch microscopist Antonie van Leeuwenhoek observed bacteria and protozoans in 1676. Leeuwenhoek ground lenses to make his own microscopes to view minuscule living things, and he recorded his research findings.

The germ theory of disease evolved in the late 1800s when Louis Pasteur and his contemporaries showed that germs cause diseases. This led to the development of microbiology. To help in diagnosing, treating, and preventing infectious disease, hospitals began using microbiologists to culture, or grow, disease-causing microorganisms from patients.

## Did You Know?

- The average person carries millions of microbes on their hands. While most are harmless, some can cause illnesses such as colds and influenza.
- The oldest bacteria is 250 million years old. It was encased in salt crystals that were discovered by scientists in 2000. They were able to revive the bacteria, and the rest is history.
- Microbes make up approximately 60 percent of the earth's biomass.
- Microbes create at least half of the oxygen on earth.
- Only 5 percent of the microbes on earth have been discovered.

Sources: MicrobeWorld.org, U.S. Department of Energy, BrightHub.com

While microbiology is generally used to benefit humans, animals, plants, and the environment, there is another side to it: bioterrorism. Infectious microorganisms in the wrong hands can be used as weapons in biological warfare.

According to the American Society for Microbiology (ASM), about one-third of the Nobel prizes in physiology or medicine awarded in the 20th century went to microbiologists.

## THE JOB

Microbiologists examine microscopic organisms (microorganisms, microbes, or germs) such as algae, bacteria, fungi, molds, protozoans, viruses, and yeasts. They are interested in the form, structure, classification, and distribution of microorganisms, as well as their interactions and relationships with each other. Microbiologists study ways that microorganisms affect human, plant, and animal life and our environment, indoors and out. They search for ways to use microorganisms to make improvements in food and drugs, as well as to understand their involvement in the spread or control of disease and pollution. For example, antibiotics are produced using bacteria or fungi, and microbes can be used to break down waste. Microorganisms are used in the making of foods like cheese and tofu, in food preservation, and in meat tenderizing processes. Flavors, colors, and added vitamins are all made from microbes.

Microbiologists work independently or as part of a team in the field collecting samples and in laboratories examining these samples. They grow bacteria in small covered dishes called Petri dishes, and they check reactions of microorganisms when introduced to physical or chemical agents in test tubes. They examine microorganisms under microscopes and keep track of their data and conduct research on computers.

Microbiologists work in the agriculture, beverage, biotechnology, chemical, education, environmental, food, manufacturing, and pharmaceutical industries, among others. They work in private companies and hospitals conducting research or developing drugs, and they work in government agencies and laboratories. Some write microbiology-related articles or books for scientific publishers.

*General microbiologists* are concerned with a broad range of study, including the structure, development, ecology, functions, and chemical changes of microorganisms.

*Medical and clinical microbiologists* have the goal of understanding, treating, and preventing diseases in humans. They explore microorganisms and infectious agents that cause various diseases, look for ways to more quickly diagnose diseases, and develop medicines to protect against diseases. Clinical microbiologists have helped prevent the spread of diseases like typhoid fever, influenza, measles, polio, whooping cough, and smallpox. Today they are trying to find cures and treatments for AIDS, cancer, cystic fibrosis, and Alzheimer's disease. Some medical and clinical microbiologists specialize even further, for example, in *virology* (the study of viruses) or *immunology* (the study of mechanisms that fight infections).

*Veterinary microbiologists* do the same for animals. It is the clinical microbiologist who analyzes biological agents in cases of suspected bioterrorism.

*Bioinformatics microbiologists* collect, manage, and study biological (especially DNA) and biochemical data at the molecular level by using computer software and hardware.

Using genetic engineering, *agricultural microbiologists* develop crops that resist the elements (e.g., frost, drought, and extreme heat) as well as diseases and pests. They also study how microorganisms affect soil and water. They try to find ways to use microorganisms to kill insects as an alternative to using unsafe pesticides. *Food microbiologists* are concerned with making safer, tastier, and healthier food products and food that is less likely to spoil or become contaminated. *Salmonella* and *Escherichia coli* (*E. coli*) are two microorganisms, commonly found in food, than can cause illness.

*Environmental microbiologists* deal with environmental contamination, perhaps in waste sites, groundwater, or other outdoor locations. They examine oil spills, hazardous waste sites, or polluted air and try to find organisms that will successfully clean up the contamination. They work to keep wildlife, rodents, and insects from transmitting infectious agents.

*Industrial microbiologists*, or *biotechnologists*, apply the principles of biology and engineering to microorganisms to develop new products (drugs, alcoholic beverages, cosmetics, and foods), monitor the safety of existing products, and oversee manufacturing processes.

*Marine microbiologists* explore microorganisms that live in the world's oceans.

## REQUIREMENTS

### High School

If you are thinking about a career in microbiology, be sure to get a well-rounded science background in high school. You should take biology, chemistry, physics, computer science, and math classes. English classes will help you develop your oral and written communication skills, which will prepare you for writing papers and public speaking.

### Postsecondary Training

An undergraduate degree in microbiological sciences is recommended. If this degree is not offered, the American Society for Microbiology suggests that you major in the biological or life sciences or in chemistry and take any available microbiology courses, such as immunology, medical microbiology, microbial physiology, mycology, pathology, and virology. In addition to microbiology classes, you will have to take courses in chemistry (e.g., organic and physical), math (algebra, calculus, and statistics), biology (cell biology and genetics), and physics.

While you may find a job in microbiology after earning a bachelor's degree, most positions in research, education, and industry require a master's degree, a Ph.D., or an M.D., which means you should be prepared to spend six or more years in school beyond high school. While you pursue your master's degree, you will conduct research under the supervision of a faculty mentor.

While in a Ph.D. program, you can expect to spend a lot of your time working in a laboratory, where you will design and conduct experiments. Many graduate students also work as teaching assistants or lab supervisors. Other experience you can gain at this level

A microbiologist (*left*), chemist (*right*), and technician study the results of a test that detects a common plant virus. *(Stephen Ausmus, Agricultural Research Service, USDA)*

includes writing grants, publishing papers, and making presentations at science conferences.

## Certification or Licensing

Certification is available in several areas. Though it is usually not necessary, it may be requested for certain positions and/or by certain states. The American College of Microbiology watches over the ASM's certification programs: the American Board of Medical Microbiology (ABMM), the American Board of Medical Laboratory Immunology (ABMLI); and the National Registry of Certified Microbiologists (NRCM). According to the American College of Microbiology, "The ABMM certifies the expertise of doctoral-level microbiologists seeking to direct public health or clinical microbiology laboratories; the ABMLI certifies the expertise of doctoral-level immunologists seeking to direct laboratories engaged in the practice of medical laboratory immunology; and the NRCM certifies professional microbiologists at the prebaccalaureate/baccalaureate, master's, and doctoral levels in biological safety; food; and pharmaceutical and medical device." The American Society for Clinical Pathology offers certification for microbiologists in the categories of specialist and technologist.

## Other Requirements

If you want to become a microbiologist, you should be inquisitive and enjoy learning, as the work involves exploring sometimes unusual or unknown microscopic life forms. Critical thinking and analytic skills are essential when observing the growth and characteristics of microorganisms so that you are able to properly evaluate problems and arrive at suitable solutions. Focus, concentration, and attention to detail are other necessary attributes. You will need to be accurate and precise in recording your research findings. Strong mathematical and computational ability will also help when it comes to recording and analyzing your data.

Since much research is conducted independently, you must be self-disciplined and enjoy working on your own. If you are more of a follower and rely on others for guidance and direction, you probably will not be able to move beyond doing very basic research. For those times when you work with a team of people or if you teach, you will need good communication skills. Clinical microbiologists have to work quickly and carefully in cases of suspected bioterrorism.

## EXPLORING

To get an idea of what microbiology is all about, try some of the ASM's assorted microbiology-related experiments at http://www .microbe.org. The ASM publishes journals dealing with different specialties in microbiology (e.g., *Applied and Environmental Microbiology, Infection and Immunity,* and *Journal of Clinical Microbiology*). By reading journals, you will learn about the field and keep up with developments.

Another way to learn about microbiology is to talk to a microbiologist. You can search for a mentor through the ASM Web site (http://www.asm.org). To gain experience working in a scientific setting, try to get a part-time job with a company whose business is related to science. Volunteer at a local hospital. The ASM suggests that you get involved in a science club or a science fair in your school or community.

You can also learn more about the field by participating in summer science programs for high school students at colleges and universities.

## EMPLOYERS

Approximately 16,900 microbiologists are employed in the United States. You can find federal government jobs with such agencies as the Environmental Protection Agency and the U.S. Department of Health and Human Services (e.g., Centers for Disease Control and Prevention, the Food and Drug Administration, and the National Institutes of Health). Jobs are also available in state departments of health and ecology.

Universities hire microbiologists to teach and to conduct research. Other employers include hospitals; medical laboratories; and biotechnology, drug and pharmaceutical, and food-processing companies. Biotechnology companies tend to be concentrated in some of the major metropolitan areas, such as Boston, New York City, Washington, D.C., Los Angeles, and San Francisco.

## STARTING OUT

While you are in college, try to find a part-time job or internship doing research in a university laboratory or with a company that hires microbiologists.

Also while you are in college, consider joining the ASM so you can take advantage of the many members-only career opportunities offered. (For student membership, you must be majoring in microbiology or a related field and not yet have earned your doctorate.) Many professional associations offer job listings at their Web sites or in their publications. During your graduate study you can attend the ASM's Kadner Institute (formerly known as the Graduate and Postdoctoral Summer Institute in Preparation for Careers in Microbiology). Other events will give you plenty of chances to network with professionals in the field. Check the ASM Web site for more in-depth information.

Upon graduation, many microbiologists become university faculty members or researchers. With a Ph.D., you may be able to obtain a postdoctoral fellowship.

## ADVANCEMENT

Microbiologists may begin as research assistants and move to supervisory positions. If properly credentialed, microbiologists may direct laboratories. Microbiologists who become instructors may move into academic administrative positions. Other advancement opportunities exist in companies, where microbiologists may move into executive positions. Experienced microbiologists are put in charge of government programs. Some microbiologists choose to start their own independent consulting businesses.

## EARNINGS

Microbiologists had median annual earnings of $66,580 in 2009, according to the U.S. Department of Labor (DOL). Salaries ranged from less than $39,150 to more than $113,150 annually. Average earnings of microbiologists employed in federal government positions were $97,264 in 2009.

In government, academic, and private industry positions, microbiologists receive the standard benefits, such as paid vacation and sick days, health and retirement plans, and tuition reimbursement.

## WORK ENVIRONMENT

Microbiologists working independently or as part of a team collect samples either indoors or outdoors, depending on where the subject (e.g., human, animal, plant, natural resource) is located. Microbiologists who collect samples outdoors will encounter varied weather and terrain. Analysis is generally carried out indoors in a sterile setting, usually a laboratory or an office. Because microbiologists often deal with disease-causing microorganisms, they must take precautions to prevent spillage or direct contact. Sometimes microbiologists have to wear protective clothing and gloves.

Microbiologists working in a hospital setting may work day or night shifts as well as weekends, since hospital laboratories generally operate around the clock to analyze germs infecting patients and to keep infections from spreading in the hospital. Independent consulting work leads to a great deal of freedom in choosing hours, projects, and clients.

## OUTLOOK

The DOL predicts that employment for microbiologists will grow as fast as the average for all careers through 2018. Areas that will also be in need of skilled microbiologists include anti-infectives, biotechnology, molecular diagnostics, mycology, and vaccines. Biofilm research is a relatively new and growing area of microbiology. This type of research concerns bacteria that band together and attach to a surface, where they grow. The field of clinical microbiology should also grow given the world's concern over bioterrorism. Additionally, as long as germs are present in our world, there should always be a need for microbiologists to detect and study them.

Microbiologists with a bachelor's or master's degree will find opportunities outside of research in sales, marketing, and research management, as well as in science and engineering technology.

## FOR MORE INFORMATION

*For information on careers in biology, contact*
**American Institute of Biological Sciences**
1444 I Street, NW, Suite 200
Washington, DC 20005-6535
Tel: 202-628-1500
http://www.aibs.org

*For information on careers in laboratory medicine, which includes microbiology, and certification, contact*
**American Society for Clinical Pathology**
33 West Monroe, Suite 1600
Chicago, IL 60603-5308
Tel: 800-267-2727
E-mail: info@ascp.org
http://www.ascp.org

*The ASM offers a wealth of resources, including microbiology news, career guidance, salary data, and an in-depth microbiology timeline.*
**American Society for Microbiology (ASM)**
1752 N Street, NW
Washington, DC 20036-2904
Tel: 202-737-3600
http://www.asm.org

*For information on bioinformatics, visit*
**Bioinformatics Organization**
http://www.bioinformatics.org

*For information on career opportunities in biotechnology, contact*
**Biotechnology Industry Organization**
1201 Maryland Avenue, SW, Suite 900
Washington, DC 20024-2149
Tel: 202-962-9200
E-mail: info@bio.org
http://www.bio.org

*For information on accredited food science programs and careers, visit the IFT Web site.*
**Institute of Food Technologists (IFT)**
525 West Van Buren, Suite 1000
Chicago, IL 60607-3830
Tel: 312-782-8424
E-mail: info@ift.org
http://www.ift.org

*The ISME site presents an introduction to the field of microbial ecology as well as job listings and details on publications.*
**International Society for Microbial Ecology (ISME)**
PO Box 40
6666 ZG Heteren, The Netherlands
http://www.isme-microbes.org

*For career information in the area of industrial microbiology and biotechnology, contact*
**Society for Industrial Microbiology**
3929 Old Lee Highway, Suite 92A
Fairfax, VA 22030-2421
Tel: 703-691-3357
E-mail: simhq@simhq.org
http://www.simhq.org

*This private organization features a collection of hands-on microbiology activities for students at different levels.*
**Waksman Foundation for Microbiology**
Swarthmore College
500 College Avenue
Swarthmore, PA 19081-1390
Tel: 610-328-8044
http://www.waksmanfoundation.org

*For access to a collection of microbiology resources, such as publications, images, and activities, check out the following Web site:*
**MicrobeLibrary.org**
http://www.microbelibrary.org

*For articles and fun facts about microbiology, visit*
**Microbe World**
http://www.microbe.org

# Naturalists

## OVERVIEW

The primary role of *naturalists* is to educate the public about the environment and maintain the natural environment on land specifically dedicated to wilderness populations. Their primary responsibilities are preserving, restoring, maintaining, and protecting a natural habitat. Among the related responsibilities in these jobs are teaching, public speaking, writing, giving scientific and ecological demonstrations, and handling public relations and administrative tasks. Naturalists may work in a variety of environments, including private nature centers; local, state, and national parks and forests; wildlife museums; and independent nonprofit conservation and restoration associations. Some of the many job titles a naturalist might hold are *wildlife manager, fish and game warden, fish and wildlife officer, land steward, wildlife biologist*, and *environmental interpreter. Natural resource managers, wildlife conservationists*, and *ecologists* sometimes perform the work of naturalists.

## HISTORY

Prior to the 17th century, there was little support for environmental preservation. Instead, wilderness was commonly seen as a vast resource to be controlled. This view began to change during the early years of the industrial revolution, when new energy resources were utilized, establishing an increasing need for petroleum, coal, natural gas, wood, and water for hydropowered energy. In England and France, for example, the rapid depletion of

## QUICK FACTS

**School Subjects**
Biology
Earth science
English

**Personal Skills**
Communication/ideas
Technical/scientific

**Work Environment**
Primarily outdoors
One location with some travel

**Minimum Education Level**
Bachelor's degree

**Salary Range**
$20,000 to $45,000 to $75,000+

**Certification or Licensing**
None available

**Outlook**
About as fast as the average

**DOT**
049

**GOE**
12.01.01

**NOC**
2121

**O*NET-SOC**
19-1031.03

forests caused by the increased use of timber for powering the new industries led to demands for forest conservation.

The United States, especially during the 19th century, saw many of its great forests razed, huge tracts of land leveled for open-pit mining and quarrying, and increased disease with the rise of air pollution from the smokestacks of factories, home chimneys, and engine exhaust. Much of the land damage occurred at the same time as a dramatic depletion of wildlife, including elk, antelope, deer, bison, and other animals of the Great Plains. Some types of bear, cougar, and wolf became extinct, as did several kinds of birds, such as the passenger pigeon. In the latter half of the 19th century, the U.S. government set up a commission to develop scientific management of fisheries, established the first national park (Yellowstone National Park in Wyoming, Idaho, and Montana), and set aside the first forest reserves. The modern conservation movement grew out of these early steps.

States also established parks and forests for wilderness conservation. Parks and forests became places where people, especially urban dwellers, could acquaint themselves with the natural settings of their ancestors. Naturalists, employed by the government, institutions of higher education, and various private concerns, were involved not only in preserving and exploring the natural reserves but also in educating the public about the remaining wilderness.

Controversy over the proper role of U.S. parks and forests began soon after their creation (and continues to this day), as the value of these natural areas for logging, recreation, and other human activities conflicted with the ecological need for preservation. President Theodore Roosevelt, a strong supporter of the conservation movement, believed nevertheless in limited industrial projects, such as dams, within the wilderness areas. Despite the controversy, the system of national parks and forests expanded throughout the 20th century. Today, the Agriculture and Interior Departments, and, to a lesser extent, the Department of Defense, have conservation responsibilities for soil, forests, grasslands, water, wildlife, and federally owned land.

In the 1960s and early 1970s, the hazards posed by pollution to both humans and the environment highlighted the importance of nature preservation and public education. Federal agencies were established, such as the Environmental Protection Agency, the Council on Environmental Quality, and the National Oceanic and Atmospheric Administration. Crucial legislation was passed, including the Wilderness Act (1964) and the Endangered Species Act (1969). Naturalists have been closely involved with these conservation efforts and

## Books to Read

Baker, Nick. *The Amateur Naturalist.* Washington, D.C.: National Geographic Books, 2005.

Barr, Nevada. *Endangered Species.* Reprint ed. New York: Berkley Books, 2008.

Brewer, Richard. *Conservancy: The Land Trust Movement in America.* Lebanon, N.H.: University Press of New England, 2004.

Grosz, Terry. *Wildlife Wars: The Life and Times of a Fish and Game Warden.* Boulder, Colo.: Johnson Books, 1999.

Hunter, Malcolm L., David Lindenmayer, and Aram Calhoun. *Saving the Earth as a Career: Advice on Becoming a Conservation Professional.* Hoboken, N.J.: Wiley-Blackwell, 2007.

Mackay, Richard. *The Atlas of Endangered Species.* Berkeley, Calif.: University of California Press, 2008.

Merchant, Carolyn, and Thomas Paterson. *Major Problems in American Environmental History.* 2d ed. Florence, Ky.: Wadsworth Publishing, 2006.

National Geographic Books. *National Geographic's Guide to the National Parks of the United States.* 6th ed. Washington, D.C.: National Geographic Books, 2009.

Schaller, George B. *A Naturalist and Other Beasts: Tales from a Life in the Field.* San Francisco: Sierra Club Books, 2007.

Williams, Ernest Herbert. *The Nature Handbook: A Guide to Observing the Great Outdoors.* New York: Oxford University Press, 2005.

Wilson, Edward O. *Naturalist.* Washington, D.C.: Island Press, 2006.

others, shouldering the responsibility to communicate to the public the importance of maintaining diverse ecosystems and to help restore or balance ecosystems under threat.

## THE JOB

Because of the impact of human populations on the environment, virtually no area in the United States (except Alaska) is truly wild. Land and the animal populations require human intervention to help battle against the human encroachment that is damaging or hindering wildlife. Naturalists work to help wildlife maintain or improve their hold in the world.

The work can be directly involved in maintaining individual populations of animals or plants, overseeing whole ecosystems, or promoting the work of those who are directly involved in the maintenance of the ecosystem. *Fish and wildlife officers* (or *fish and game wardens*) work to preserve and restore the animal populations, including migratory birds that may only be part of the environment temporarily. *Wildlife managers* and *range conservationists* oversee the combination of plants and animals in their territories.

Fish and wildlife officers and wardens study, assist, and help regulate the populations of fish, hunted animals, and protected animals throughout the United States. They may work directly in the parks and reserves, or they may oversee a region within a particular state, even if there are no park lands there. Fish and game wardens control the hunting and fishing of wild populations to make sure that the populations are not overharvested during a season. They monitor the populations of each species off season as well as make sure the species is thriving but is not overpopulating and running the risk of starvation or territory damage. Most people hear about the fish and game wardens when a population of animals has overgrown its territory and needs either to be culled (selectively hunted) or moved. Usually this occurs with the deer population, but it can also apply to predator animals such as the coyote or fox, or scavenger animals such as the raccoon. Because the practice of culling animal populations arouses controversy, the local press usually gives wide coverage to such situations.

The other common time to hear about wildlife wardens is when poaching is uncovered locally. Poaching can be hunting or fishing an animal out of season or hunting or fishing a protected animal. Although we think of poachers in the African plains hunting lions and elephants, poaching is common in the United States for animals such as mountain lions, brown bears, eagles, and wolves. Game wardens target and arrest poachers; punishment can include prison sentences and steep fines.

Wildlife managers, *range managers*, and *conservationists* work to maintain the plant and animal life in a given area. Wildlife managers can work in small local parks or enormous national parks. Range managers work on ranges that have a combination of domestic livestock and wild population. The U.S. government has leased and permitted farmers to graze and raise livestock on federally held ranges, although this program is under increasing attack by environmentalists. Range managers must ensure that both the domestic and wild populations are living side by side successfully. They make sure that the population of predatory wild animals does not increase enough to deplete the livestock and that the livestock does not overgraze the land and eliminate essential food for the wild animals. Range managers and conservationists must test soil and water for nutrients and pollution, count plant and animal populations in every season, and keep in contact with farmers using the land for reports of attacks on livestock or the presence of disease.

Wildlife managers also balance the needs of the humans using or traveling through the land they supervise and the animals that live in or travel through that same land. They keep track of the populations of animals and plants and provide food and water when it is lacking naturally. This may involve airdrops of hay and grain during winter months to deer, moose, or elk populations in remote reaches of a national forest, or digging and filling a water reservoir for animals during a drought.

Naturalists in all these positions often have administrative duties such as supervising staff members and volunteers, raising funds (particularly for independent nonprofit organizations), writing grant applications, taking and keeping records and statistics, and maintaining public relations. They may write articles for local or national publications to inform and educate the public about their location or a specific project. They may be interviewed by journalists for reports concerning their site or their work.

Nature walks are often given to groups as a way of educating people about the land and the work that goes into revitalizing and maintaining it. Tourists, schoolchildren, amateur conservationists and naturalists, social clubs, and retirees commonly attend these walks. On a nature walk, the naturalist may point out specific plants and animals, identify rocks, and discuss soil composition or the natural history of the area (including special environmental strengths and problems). The naturalist may even discuss the indigenous people of the area, especially in terms of how they adapted to the unique aspects of their particular environment. Because such a variety of topics may be brought up, the naturalist must be an environmental generalist, familiar with such subjects as biology, botany, geology, geography, meteorology, anthropology, and history.

Demonstrations, exhibits, and classes are ways that the naturalist can educate the public about the environment. For example, to help children understand oil spills, the naturalist may set up a simple demonstration showing that oil and water do not mix. Sometimes the natural setting already provides an exhibit for the naturalist. Dead fish, birds, and other animals found in a park may help demonstrate the natural life cycle and the process of decomposition. Instruction may also be given on outdoor activities, such as hiking and camping.

For some naturalists, preparing educational materials is a large part of their job. Brochures, fact sheets, pamphlets, and newsletters may be written for people visiting the park or nature center. Materials might also be sent to area residents in an effort to gain public support.

One aspect of protecting any natural area involves communicating facts and debunking myths about how to respect the area and the flora and fauna that inhabit it. Another aspect involves tending managed areas to promote a diversity of plants and animals. This may mean introducing trails and footpaths that provide easy yet noninvasive access for the public; it may mean cordoning off an area to prevent foot traffic from ruining a patch of rare moss; or it may mean instigating a letter-writing campaign to drum up support for legislation to protect a specific area, plant, or animal. It may be easy to get support for protecting the snowshoe rabbit; it is harder to make the public understand the need to preserve and maintain a bat cave.

Some naturalists, such as *directors of nature centers or conservation organizations*, have massive administrative responsibilities. They might recruit volunteers and supervise staff, organize long- and short-term program goals, and handle record keeping and the budget. To raise money, naturalists may need to speak publicly on a regular basis, write grant proposals, and organize and attend scheduled fund-raising activities and community meetings. Naturalists also try to increase public awareness and support by writing press releases and organizing public workshops, conferences, seminars, meetings, and hearings. In general, naturalists must be available as resources for educating and advising the community.

## REQUIREMENTS

### High School

If you are interested in this field, you should take a number of basic science courses, including biology, chemistry, and earth science. Botany courses and clubs are helpful, since they provide direct experience monitoring plant growth and health. Animal care experience, usually obtained through volunteer work, also is helpful. Take English courses in high school to improve your writing skills, which you will use when writing grant proposals and conducting research.

### Postsecondary Training

An undergraduate degree in environmental, physical, or natural sciences is generally the minimum educational requirement for becoming a naturalist. Common college majors are biology, forestry, wildlife management, natural resource and park management, natural resources, botany, zoology, chemistry, natural history, and environmental science. Course work in economics, history, anthropology, English, international studies, and communication arts are also helpful.

Graduate education is increasingly required for employment as a naturalist, particularly for upper-level positions. A master's degree in natural science or natural resources is the minimum requirement for supervisory or administrative roles in many of the nonprofit agencies, and several positions require either a doctorate or several years of experience in the field. For positions in agencies with international sites, work abroad is necessary and can be obtained through volunteer positions such as those with the Peace Corps or in paid positions assisting in site administration and management.

**Other Requirements**

If you are considering a career in this field, you should like working outdoors, as most naturalists spend the majority of their time outside in all kinds of weather. However, along with the desire to work in and with the natural world, you need to be capable of communicating with the human world as well. Excellent writing skills are helpful in preparing educational materials and grant proposals.

Seemingly unrelated skills in this field, such as engine repair and basic carpentry, can be essential to managing a post. Because of the remote locations of many of the work sites, self-sufficiency in operating and maintaining the equipment allows the staff to lose fewer days because of equipment breakdown.

## EXPLORING

One of the best ways to learn about the job of a naturalist is to volunteer at one of the many national and state parks or nature centers. These institutions often recruit volunteers for outdoor work. College students, for example, are sometimes hired to work as summer or part-time nature guides. Outdoor recreation and training organizations, such as Outward Bound (http://www.outwardbound.org) and the National Outdoor Leadership School (http://www.nols.edu), are especially good resources. Most volunteer positions, though, require a high school diploma and some college credit.

You should also consider college internship programs. In addition, conservation programs and organizations throughout the country and the world offer opportunities for volunteer work in a wide variety of areas, including working with the public, giving lectures and guided tours, and working with others to build or maintain an ecosystem. For more frequent, up-to-date information, you can read newsletters, such as *Environmental Career Opportunities* (http:// www.ecojobs.com), that post internship and job positions. The Web site, Environmental Career Center (http://environmentalcareer.com) also offers job listings.

Read books and magazines about nature and the career of naturalists. One interesting publication is *The American Naturalist*, published by the University of Chicago Press for the American Society of Naturalists. Visit http://www.journals.uchicago.edu/AN/home.html to read sample articles.

## EMPLOYERS

Naturalists may be employed by state agencies such as departments of wildlife, departments of fish and game, or departments of natural resources. They may work at the federal level for the U.S. Fish and Wildlife Service or the National Park Service. Naturalists may also work in the private sector for such employers as nature centers, arboretums, and botanical gardens.

## STARTING OUT

If you hope to become a park employee, the usual method of entry is through part-time or seasonal employment for the first several jobs, then a full-time position. Because it is difficult to get experience before completing a college degree, and because seasonal employment is common, you should prepare to seek supplemental income for your first few years in the field.

International experience is helpful with agencies that work beyond the U.S. borders. This can be through the Peace Corps or other volunteer organizations that work with local populations on land and habitat management or restoration. Other volunteer experience is available through local restoration programs on sites in your area. Organizations such as The Nature Conservancy (http://www.nature .org), The Trust for Public Land (http://www.tpl.org), and many others buy land to restore, and these organizations rely extensively on volunteer labor for stewarding and working the land. Rescue and release centers work with injured and abandoned wildlife to rehabilitate them. Opportunities at these centers can include banding wild animals for tracking, working with injured or adolescent animals for release training, and adapting unreleasable animals to educational programs and presentations.

## ADVANCEMENT

In some settings, such as small nature centers, there may be little room for advancement. In larger organizations, experience and additional education can lead to increased responsibility and pay. Among the higher-level positions is that of director, handling supervisory, administrative, and public relations tasks.

Advancement into upper-level management and supervisory positions usually requires a graduate degree, although people with a graduate degree and no work experience will still have to start in nearly entry-level positions. So you can either work a few years and then return to school to get an advanced degree or complete your education and start in the same position as you would have without the degree. The advanced degree will allow you eventually to move further up in the organizational structure.

## EARNINGS

Earnings for naturalists are influenced by several factors, including the naturalist's specific job (for example, a wildlife biologist, a water and soil conservationist, or a game manager), the employer (for example, a state or federal agency), and the naturalist's experience and education. The U.S. Fish and Wildlife Service reports that biologists working for this department have starting salaries at the GS-5 to GS-7 levels on the federal government pay scale. In 2010, biologists at the GS-5 pay level earned annual salaries that ranged from $27,431 to $35,657, and those at the GS-7 level earned annual salaries that ranged from $33,979 to $44,176. The U.S. Fish and Wildlife Service further reports that biologists can expect to advance to GS-11 or GS-12 levels. In 2010, basic yearly pay at these levels was $50,287 and $60,274, respectively. In general, those working for state agencies have somewhat lower earnings, particularly at the entry level. And, again, the specific job a naturalist performs affects earnings. For example, the U.S. Department of Labor reports that conservation scientists had a median annual salary of $60,160 in 2009. However, some conservation workers put in 40-hour weeks and make less than $20,000 annually. As with other fields, management positions are among the highest paying. Salaries for managers may range from $45,000 to $75,000 or more annually. Keep in mind, though, that this position and these earnings are at the top of the field. The candidate who meets the qualifications for this position would have extensive experience and be responsible for, among other things, managing research programs statewide, hiring lower-level managers, prioritizing and directing research, and acting as the department representative to other government agencies and public groups.

For some positions, housing and vehicles may be provided. Other benefits, depending on employer, may include health insurance, vacation time, and retirement plans.

## WORK ENVIRONMENT

Field naturalists spend a majority of their working hours outdoors. Depending on the location, the naturalist must work in a wide variety of weather conditions: from frigid cold to sweltering heat to torrential rain. Remote sites are common, and long periods of working either in isolation or in small teams is not uncommon for field research and management. Heavy lifting, hauling, working with machinery and hand tools, digging, planting, harvesting, and tracking may fall to the naturalist working in the field. One wildlife manager in Montana spent every daylight hour for several days in a row literally running up and down snow-covered mountains, attempting to tranquilize and collar a mountain lion. Clearly, this can be a physically demanding job.

Indoor work includes scheduling, planning, and classroom teaching. Data gathering and maintaining logs and records are required for many jobs. Naturalists may need to attend and speak at local community meetings. They may have to read detailed legislative bills to analyze the impact of legislation before it becomes law.

Those in supervisory positions, such as directors, are often so busy with administrative and organizational tasks that they may spend little of their workday outdoors. Work that includes guided tours and walks through nature areas is frequently seasonal and usually dependent on daily visitors.

Full-time naturalists usually work about 35 to 40 hours per week. Overtime is often required, and for those naturalists working in areas visited by campers, camping season is extremely busy and can require much overtime. Wildlife and range managers may be on call during storms and severe weather. Seasonal work, such as burn season for land managers and stewards, may require overtime and frequent weekend work.

Naturalists have special occupational hazards, such as working with helicopters, small airplanes, all-terrain vehicles, and other modes of transport through rugged landscapes and into remote regions. Adverse weather conditions and working in rough terrain make illness and injury more likely. Naturalists must be able to get along with the variety of people using the area and may encounter armed individuals who are poaching or otherwise violating the law.

Working as a naturalist also provides a number of unique benefits. Most prominent is the chance to live and work in some of the most beautiful places in the world. For many individuals, the lower salaries are offset by the recreational and lifestyle opportunities afforded by living and working in such scenic areas. In general, occupational stress is low, and most naturalists appreciate the opportunity to continually learn about and work to improve the environment.

## OUTLOOK

The employment for naturalists is expected to grow about as fast as the average through 2018. While a growing public concern about environmental issues may cause an increased demand for naturalists, this trend could be offset by government cutbacks in funding for nature programs. Reduced government spending on education may indirectly affect the demand for naturalists, as school districts would have less money to spend on outdoor education and recreation. Despite the limited number of available positions, the number of well-qualified applicants is expected to remain high.

## FOR MORE INFORMATION

*For information on careers, contact*
**American Society of Naturalists**
E-mail: asn@press.uchicago.edu
http://www.amnat.org

*For information about career opportunities, contact*
**Bureau of Land Management**
U.S. Department of the Interior
1849 C Street, Room 5665
Washington, DC 20240-0001
Tel: 202-208-3801
http://www.blm.gov

*For information on environmental expeditions, contact*
**Earthwatch Institute**
114 Western Avenue
Boston, MA 02134-1037
Tel: 800-776-0188
E-mail: info@earthwatch.org
http://www.earthwatch.org

*This group offers internships and fellowships for college and graduate students with an interest in environmental issues. For information, contact*
**Friends of the Earth**
1100 15th Street, NW, 11th Floor
Washington, DC 20005-1707
Tel: 877-843-8687
http://www.foe.org

*For information on a variety of conservation programs, contact*
**National Wildlife Federation**
11100 Wildlife Center Drive
Reston, VA 20190-5362
Tel: 800-822-9919
http://www.nwf.org

*For information on volunteer opportunities, contact*
**Student Conservation Association**
689 River Road
PO Box 550
Charlestown, NH 03603-0550
Tel: 603-543-1700
E-mail: ask-us@thesca.org
http://www.thesca.org

*For information on careers, contact*
**U.S. Fish and Wildlife Service**
U.S. Department of the Interior
Division of Human Resources
4401 North Fairfax Drive, Mailstop: 2000
Arlington, VA 22203-1610
Tel: 800-344-9453
http://www.fws.gov/jobs

# Oceanographers

## OVERVIEW

*Oceanographers* obtain information about the ocean through observations, surveys, and experiments. They study the biological, physical, and chemical composition of the ocean and the geological structure of the seabed. They also analyze phenomena involving the water itself, the atmosphere above it, the land beneath it, and the coastal borders. They study acoustical properties of water so that a comprehensive and unified picture of the ocean's behavior may be developed.

## HISTORY

People have studied the oceans of the world and the organisms that live in them for thousands of years. In fact, the Greek philosopher Aristotle wrote *Historia Animalium*, the first treatise on marine biology in 325 B.C.

Scientists, explorers, and mariners continued to study the oceans for the next two thousand years, but it was not until the 1800s that the seeds of modern oceanography were planted as a result of ocean explorations by scientists from a variety of countries. Some noteworthy expeditions include those of Sir John Ross in the Arctic Ocean (1817–18), Charles Darwin (1831–36) to many regions in the Pacific Ocean, Sir James Ross (the nephew of Sir John Ross) to Antarctica (1839–43), Charles Wyville Thompson and John Murray to all the oceans of the world except the Arctic (1872–76), and Alexander Agassiz (1877–80) to areas of the South Pacific. Other significant developments that fueled the work of early oceanographers were the founding of the first U.S. marine station on Penikese Island in Massachusetts in

1873; the construction of the USS *Albatross* (1884), which was used specifically to conduct scientific research at sea; the establishment of the Marine Biological Laboratory at Woods Hole, Massachusetts (1888); the establishment of the International Council for the Exploration of the Sea (1902), which studied ocean conditions that affected fisheries in the North Atlantic; and the establishment of the Scripps Institution of Biological Research (now known as the Scripps Institution of Oceanography) in 1903.

From 1925 to 1927, a German research expedition aboard the *Meteor* studied the physical oceanography of the Atlantic Ocean. This expedition marked the beginning of the modern age of oceanographic investigation, according to *Invitation to Oceanography*, by Paul R. Pinet.

Today, oceanographers continue to study the world's oceans. They are in strong demand to study and find solutions to global warming, pollution, overfishing, and declining species diversity; study the vast array of life in the sea; and find and utilize ocean resources for the benefit of humanity.

## THE JOB

Oceanography is a highly interdisciplinary science that covers all aspects of ocean study and exploration. It draws on the sciences of chemistry, biology, geology, botany, zoology, meteorology, physics, fluid mechanics, and applied mathematics. There are four main oceanography specialties: *biological*, *chemical*, *geological*, and *physical*.

*Biological oceanographers* study the many forms of life in the sea. Unlike *marine biologists*, who study the physiology and habits of individual organisms, biological oceanographers strive to understand the relationship between living organisms and their environment. They study patterns in population density, life cycles, physical and chemical factors that influence the distribution and volume of ocean life, and the cycling of nutrients (nitrogen, phosphorus, etc.) through the marine food chain. They also examine the distribution of plants and animals through the ocean, the relationships between different organisms, and the impact of human behavior on ocean life. Biological oceanographers conduct research in the field. During field research they might travel on a research vessel and conduct research by lowering instruments and water sampling gear into the ocean from the ship or they may dive into the water to observe and gather samples of marine organisms such as zooplankton. They travel deep beneath the ocean surface in underwater submersible vehicles to study biological communities, such as those that live near deep-sea hydrothermal vents.

*Chemical oceanographers* study the chemical characteristics of the ocean and the chemical interactions that occur between the ocean, the atmosphere, and the sea floor. They study the impact these chemical interactions have on living organisms and man-made materials. They study the effects of pollution (runoff of sewage, oil, fuel, and agricultural chemicals) on the ocean. For example, a chemical oceanographer employed by the Environmental Protection Agency might conduct research to identify toxic compounds in sediments gathered from the ocean floor. Once the toxic compound is pinpointed, it can be traced to its source (illegal chemical dumping, etc.) and future pollution can be prevented. Other chemical oceanographers study carbon cycling in the world's oceans. This research helps scientists determine the degree and speed of global warming and its effects on ocean environments and human populations. One major recent focus of chemical oceanographers is on the role seawater temperature and salinity play in global climate change. Chemical oceanographers also may investigate ocean resources that may be useful for fuel, food, or medicine.

There are several subspecialties in the field of chemical oceanography. *Marine chemists* study the past and current chemical composition of seawater. They try to protect the oceans from pollution and seek out ocean resources that may have medicinal properties. *Marine geochemists* are concerned with the chemical composition of, and the changes in, minerals and rocks. They also study the role that organisms play in the formation and changing of geological features. *Marine biogeochemists* study the geological, physical, and biological processes that fuel chemical cycling in ocean systems. *Atmospheric chemists* study chemicals in the atmosphere and their relationship with the oceans.

*Geological oceanographers* study the contour and materials of the seafloor (rocks, fossils, etc.) in order to draw conclusions about ocean circulation, climate, seafloor spreading, plate tectonics, and the ocean's geological features. They study physical features such as underwater mountains, rises and ridges, trenches, valleys, abyssal hills, and the ocean crust. They take sediment samples from the ocean floor to learn about the history of oceanic circulation and climates. Geological oceanographers study the physical and chemical properties of sediment samples, as well as their age, distribution, and origin—to learn more about historical and ongoing geological processes. They attempt to understand the origin of volcanoes and earthquakes and the gradual movement of the earth's surface. They also study erosional processes and the formation of hydrothermal vents. Geological oceanography is considered to be one of the most diverse earth sciences fields, with many subspecialties. Some specializations include seismology, ocean drilling, ocean mining and oil and gas exploration, coastal geology, paleontology, geochronology, and petrology.

*Physical oceanographers* examine physical forces and features within the ocean. They observe and record the currents, temperatures, density, salinity, and acoustical characteristics of the ocean. Physical oceanographers are also concerned with the interaction between the ocean and the atmosphere, land, freshwater sources such as rivers, and the seafloor. A physical oceanographer might, for instance, try to determine how the ocean influences the climate or weather or affects a certain stretch of coastline. Some of the issues studied by physical oceanographers include weather and climate trends (including global warming), ocean pollution, the decline of ocean fisheries (which have crashed as a result of overfishing, pollution, and other factors), and algal blooms (often known as red tides) that can harm humans and ocean ecosystems.

In addition to field research, oceanographers spend a lot of time indoors in laboratories and offices analyzing data, samples, and specimens gathered during field research. Technology is also allowing oceanographers to conduct research without ever leaving their offices. Satellites, airborne sensors, programmable buoys, and other remote sensing devices are just a few of the technologies oceanographers use in their work. They also use mathematical modeling software that helps them answer questions that can not be completely answered by hands-on research, such as the effects that global warming or pollution will have on the oceans over a long period of time.

Many oceanographers are employed at colleges and universities. They teach classes and conduct research in laboratories and in the field. Some write textbooks and articles about the field.

## REQUIREMENTS

### High School

Because a college degree is required for beginning positions in oceanography, you should take four years of college preparatory courses while in high school. Science courses, including geology, biology, and chemistry, and math classes, such as algebra, trigonometry, and statistics, are especially important to take. Because your work will involve a great deal of research and documentation, take English classes to improve your research and communication skills. In addition, take computer science classes because you will be using computers throughout your professional life.

## Postsecondary Training

A bachelor's degree is the minimum educational requirement to enter the field, but most employers require a master's degree in one of the four oceanography specialties, marine science, or a related field. In college, a broad program covering the basic sciences with a major in physics, chemistry, biology, or geology is desirable. In addition, you should include courses in field research or laboratory work in oceanography where available. Graduate work in oceanography is required for most positions in research and teaching. More than 100 institutions offer programs in marine studies, and more than 35 universities have graduate programs leading to a doctoral degree in oceanography.

As a college student preparing for graduate work in oceanography, you should take mathematics through differential and integral calculus and at least one year each of chemistry and physics, biology or geology, and a modern foreign language.

Many oceanography students participate in internships or work as teaching assistants while in college to gain hands-on experience in the field. The American Society of Limnology and Oceanography offers a list of internships at its Web site, http://www.aslo.org.

## Certification or Licensing

Oceanographers may scuba dive when conducting research. Organizations such as PADI provide basic certification (see For More Information for contact details).

## Other Requirements

Personal traits helpful to a career in oceanography are a strong interest in science, particularly the physical and earth sciences; an interest in situations involving activities of an abstract and creative nature (observing nature, performing experiments, creating objects); an interest in outdoor activities such as hunting, fishing, swimming, boating, or animal care; an interest in scholarly activities (reading, researching, writing); and other interests that cut across the traditional academic boundaries of biology, chemistry, and physics.

You should have above-average aptitudes in verbal, numerical, and spatial abilities. Prospective oceanographers should also be able to discriminate detail among objects in terms of their shape, size, color, or markings.

## EXPLORING

Read books and visit Web sites about oceanography. One book suggestion is *Oceanography: An Invitation to Marine Science*, 7th edition, by Tom S. Garrison. Your school or community librarian can suggest many other resources. Visit the Sea Grant Marine Careers Web site (http://www.marinecareers.net) for links to information on internships, volunteerships, and other activities, such as sea camps.

Obviously, if you live near coastal regions, you will have an easier time becoming familiar with oceans and ocean life than if you are land-bound. However, some institutions offer work or leisure-time experiences that provide participants with opportunities to explore particular aspects of oceanography. Possible opportunities include work in marine or conservation fisheries or on board seagoing vessels or field experiences in studying rocks, minerals, or aquatic life. If you live or travel near one of the oceanography research centers, such as Woods Hole Oceanographic Institution on Cape Cod, the University of Miami's Rosenstiel School of Marine and Atmospheric Science, or the Scripps Institution of Oceanography in California, you should plan to spend some time learning about their activities and studying their exhibits.

Volunteer work for students is often available with research teams, nonprofit organizations, and public centers such as aquariums. If you do not live near water, try to find summer internships, camps, or programs that involve travel to a coastal area.

You can help pave your way into the field by learning all you can about the geology, atmosphere, and plant and animal life of the area where you live, regardless of whether water is present.

## EMPLOYERS

At present, the government employs approximately 23 percent of oceanographers. Another 40 percent hold academic positions. The remainder work for private industry and not-for-profit environmental organizations.

Within the federal government, oceanographers are employed by the National Science Foundation; Departments of Commerce (National Oceanic and Atmospheric Administration), Defense, Energy, and Interior (National Park Service, Minerals Management Service); National Aeronautics and Space Administration; Environmental Protection Agency; Biological Resources Discipline of the U.S. Geological Survey; Naval Oceanographic Office; Naval Research Laboratory; and Office of Naval Research.

Private sector oceanographers may be engaged in research and development or resource management. For example, a biological oceanographer might work for a pharmaceutical company, trying to identify chemicals that could lead to the development of new medicines.

While positions in private industry tend to offer higher compensation than academic or governmental positions, industry scientists are expected to study topics of concern to their employers. Oceanographers who work for universities usually have more freedom to pursue the questions and ideas that interest them.

## STARTING OUT

Most college career services offices are staffed to help you find positions in business and industry after you graduate. Often positions can be found through friends, relatives, or college professors or through the college's career services office by application and interview. College and university assistantships, instructorships, and professorships are usually obtained by recommendation of your major professor or department chairperson. In addition, internships with the government or private industry during college can often lead to permanent employment after graduation. Additionally, the Marine Technology Society, American Society of Limnology and Oceanography, and The Oceanography Society offer job listings at their Web sites.

## ADVANCEMENT

Starting oceanography positions usually involve working as a laboratory or research assistant, with on-the-job training in applying oceanographic principles to the problems at hand. Some beginning oceanographers with Ph.D.'s may qualify for college teaching or research positions. Experienced personnel, particularly those with advanced graduate work or doctorates, can become supervisors or administrators. Such positions involve considerable responsibility in planning and policymaking or policy interpretation. Those who achieve top-level oceanographer positions may plan and supervise research projects involving a number of workers, or they may be in charge of an oceanographic laboratory or aquarium.

## EARNINGS

While marine scientists are richly rewarded in nonmaterial ways for their diverse and exciting work with the sea, they almost never become wealthy by American standards. Salaries depend on education, experience, and chosen discipline. Supply and demand issues along with where you work also come into play. Some examples of jobs in the marine sciences that presently pay more than the average include physical oceanography, marine technology and engineering, and computer modeling.

According to the U.S. Department of Labor (DOL), in 2009, salaries for geoscientists (an occupational group that includes geologists, geophysicists, and oceanographers) ranged from less than $43,140 to more than $161,260, with a median of $81,220. The average salary for experienced oceanographers working for the federal government was $105,671 in 2009.

In 2009, the average salary for those who worked as assistant professors averaged $63,827, while associate professors earned $76,147, according to the American Association of University Professors.

In addition to their regular salaries, oceanographers may supplement their incomes with fees earned from consulting, lecturing, and publishing their findings. As highly trained scientists, oceanographers usually enjoy good benefits, such as health insurance and retirement plans offered by their employers.

## WORK ENVIRONMENT

Oceanographers in shore stations, laboratories, and research centers work five-day, 40-hour weeks. Occasionally, they serve a longer shift, particularly when a research experiment demands around-the-clock surveillance. Such assignments may also involve unusual working hours, depending on the nature of the research or the purpose of the trip. Trips at sea mean time away from home for periods extending from a few days to several months. Sea expeditions may be physically demanding and present an entirely different way of life: living on board a ship. Weather conditions may impose some hazards during these assignments. Choosing to engage in underwater research may mean a more adventuresome and hazardous way of life than in other occupations. It is wise to discover early whether or not life at sea appeals to you so that you may pursue appropriate jobs within the oceanography field.

Many jobs in oceanography, however, exist in laboratories, offices, and aquariums, with little time spent underwater or at sea. Many oceanographers are needed to analyze samples brought to land from sea; to plan, develop, and organize seafaring trips from land; and to teach. Oceanographers who work in colleges or universities get the added benefit of the academic calendar, which provides time off for travel or research.

## OUTLOOK

The DOL predicts that employment for all geoscientists (including oceanographers) will grow faster than the average for all occupations through 2018. Funding for graduate students and professional positions is expected to increase during the coming decade in the areas of global climate change, environmental research and management, fisheries science, and marine biomedical and pharmaceutical research programs. Despite this prediction, competition for top positions will be strong. Oceanographers who have Ph.D.'s, speak a foreign language, and who are willing to work abroad will have especially strong employment prospects.

In recent years, the largest demand in oceanography and marine-related fields was for physical and chemical oceanographers and ocean engineers, according to The Oceanographic Society. Demand and supply, however, are difficult to predict and can change according to the world market situation; for example, the state of the offshore oil market can affect demand for geological and geophysical oceanographers.

The growth of technology will continue to create and expand job opportunities for those interested in the marine sciences. As ways of collecting and analyzing data become more advanced, many more research positions are opening up for microbiologists, geneticists, and biochemists, fields that were limited by the capabilities of past technology but are now rapidly expanding. All these fields can have ties to the marine biological sciences. In general, oceanographers that also have training in other sciences or in engineering will probably have better opportunities for employment than those with training limited to oceanography.

The Oceanography Society says the growing interest in understanding and protecting the environment will also create new jobs. Careers related to fisheries resources, including basic research in biology and chemistry, as well as mariculture and sea ranching, will also increase. Because the oceans hold vast resources of commercially valuable minerals, employment opportunities will come from pharmaceutical and biotechnology companies and others interested in mining these substances for potential "miracle drugs" and other commercial uses. Continued deep-sea exploration made possible by underwater robotics and autonomous seacraft may also create more market opportunities for underwater research, with perhaps more international than U.S.-based employment potential.

## FOR MORE INFORMATION

*For education and career information, contact the following organizations:*

**Acoustical Society of America**
Two Huntington Quadrangle, Suite 1NO1
Melville, NY 11747-4502
Tel: 516-576-2360
E-mail: asa@aip.org
http://asa.aip.org

**American Geophysical Union**
2000 Florida Avenue, NW
Washington, DC 20009-1277
Tel: 800-966-2481
http://www.agu.org

*This organization for diving scientists stresses diving safety and offers internships for college students.*

**American Academy of Underwater Scientists**
Dauphin Island Sea Lab
101 Bienville Boulevard
Dauphin Island, AL 36528-4603
Tel: 251-591-3775
E-mail: aaus@disl.org
http://www.aaus.org

*For information on fisheries science, contact*

**American Fisheries Society**
5410 Grosvenor Lane
Bethesda, MD 20814-2144
Tel: 301-897-8616
http://www.fisheries.org

*The Education section of the institute's Web site has information on careers in biology.*

**American Institute of Biological Sciences**
1444 I Street, NW, Suite 200
Washington, DC 20005-6535

Tel: 202-628-1500
http://www.aibs.org

*Visit the society's Web site for information on careers and education.*
**American Society of Limnology and Oceanography**
5400 Bosque Boulevard, Suite 680
Waco, TX 76710-4446
Tel: 800-929-2756
E-mail: business@aslo.org
http://www.aslo.org

*To purchase the booklet* Education and Training Programs in Oceanography and Related Fields, *contact*
**Marine Technology Society**
5565 Sterrett Place, Suite 108
Columbia, MD 21044-2606
Tel: 410-884-5330
http://www.mtsociety.org

*For information on oceanography, contact*
**National Oceanic and Atmospheric Administration**
U.S. Department of Commerce
1401 Constitution Avenue, NW, Room 5128
Washington, DC 20230-0001
http://www.noaa.gov

*Contact the society for ocean news and information on membership.*
**The Oceanography Society**
PO Box 1931
Rockville, MD 20849-1931
Tel: 301-251-7708
E-mail: info@tos.org
http://www.tos.org

*For information on diving instruction and certification, contact*
**PADI**
30151 Tomas Street
Rancho Santa Margarita, CA 92688-2125
Tel: 800-729-7234
http://www.padi.com

*For links to career information and sea programs, visit the following Web sites:*

**Careers in Oceanography, Marine Science, and Marine Biology**
http://ocean.peterbrueggeman.com/career.html

**Sea Grant Marine Careers**
http://www.marinecareers.net

**WomenOceanographers.org**
http://www.womenoceanographers.org

# Toxicologists

## OVERVIEW

*Toxicologists* design and conduct studies to determine the potential toxicity of substances to humans, plants, and animals. They provide information on the hazards of these substances to the federal government, private businesses, and the public. Toxicologists may suggest alternatives to using products that contain dangerous amounts of toxins, often by testifying at official hearings.

## HISTORY

The study of the effects of poisons (toxins) began in the 1500s, when doctors documented changes in body tissues of people who died after a long illness. Although research was hampered by the lack of sophisticated research equipment, physicians and scientists continued to collect information on the causes and effects of various diseases over the next 300 years.

As microscopes and other forms of scientific equipment improved, scientists were able to study in greater detail the impacts of chemicals on the human body and the causes of disease. In the mid-1800s, Rudolf Virchow, a German scientist considered to be the founder of pathology (the study of diseased body tissue), began to unlock the mystery of many diseases by studying tissues at the cellular level. His research of diseased cells helped pathologists pinpoint the paths diseases take in the body.

With society's increasing dependence on chemicals (for example, in agriculture, industry, and medicine) and growing use of prescribed (and illegal) drugs, the study of the impact of these potential toxins on public health and environmental quality has

**School Subjects**
Biology
Chemistry
Mathematics

**Personal Skills**
Helping/teaching
Technical/scientific

**Work Environment**
Primarily indoors
Primarily one location

**Minimum Education Level**
Bachelor's degree

**Salary Range**
$35,000 to $70,000 to
$200,000+

**Certification or Licensing**
Recommended

**Outlook**
About as fast as the average

**DOT**
041

**GOE**
N/A

**NOC**
2121

**O*NET-SOC**
N/A

become more important. The toxicologist's role in determining the extent of a problem, as well as suggesting possible alternatives or antidotes, plays an important role in society. Toxicologists act as consultants on developing long-term solutions to problems such as air and water pollution, the dumping of toxic waste into landfills, and the recognition of an unusual reaction to a pharmaceutical drug.

## THE JOB

As scientists, toxicologists are concerned with the detection and effects of toxins, as well as developing methods to treat intoxication (poisonings). A primary objective of a toxicologist is to protect consumers by reducing the risks of accidental exposure to poisons. Toxicologists investigate the many areas in which our society uses potential toxins and documents their impact. For example, a toxicologist may chemically analyze a fish in a local lake to read for mercury, a harmful toxin to humans if consumed in high enough levels. This reading is reported to government or industry officials, who, in turn, write up a legal policy setting the maximum level of mercury that manufacturing companies can release without contaminating nearby fish and endangering consumers.

On many projects, a toxicologist may be part of a research team, such as at a poison control center or a research laboratory. *Clinical toxicologists* may work to help save emergency drug overdose victims. *Industrial toxicologists* and *academic toxicologists* work on solving long-term issues, such as studying the toxic effects of cigarettes. They may focus on research and development, working to improve and speed up testing methods without sacrificing safety. Toxicologists use the most modern equipment, such as electron microscopes, atomic absorption spectrometers, and mass spectrometers, and they study new research instrumentation that may help with sophisticated research.

Industrial toxicologists work for private companies, testing new products for potential poisons. For example, before a new cosmetic product can be sold, it must be tested according to strict guidelines. Toxicologists oversee this testing, which is often done on laboratory animals. These toxicologists may apply the test article ingredients topically, orally, or by injection. They test the results through observation, blood analysis, and dissection and detailed pathologic examination. Research results are used for labeling and packaging instructions to ensure that customers use the product safely. Although animal experimentation has created a great deal of controversy with animal-rights supporters, humane procedures are stressed throughout toxicology studies.

*Forensic toxicologists* are specialists who detect and identify the presence of poisons or legal or illegal drugs in an individual's body. The best-known part of the forensic toxicologist's job is seeking to determine whether illegal or prescription drugs, poisons, metals, alcohol, gases (such as carbon dioxide), or other chemicals contributed to a person's death. In doing this, the toxicologist works with law enforcement officers, other forensic scientists, and crime scene investigators. The toxicologist performs tests on body fluid and tissue samples received from the forensic pathologist and then assists with the interpretation of the findings. Most forensic toxicology laboratories routinely screen for perhaps a few hundred to a few thousand chemical compounds. Other forensic toxicologists help investigate crimes in which an individual's drug or alcohol use is a factor in the crime or may be a defense. This involves the same application of techniques as in a death investigation, but it usually involves lower concentrations of drugs, requiring more sensitive testing to produce precise results. Forensic toxicologists also work on cases involving the poisoning of animals, the use of drugs to facilitate sexual assault, and illicit and performance-enhancing drug use in sports, from track and field and the well-known team sports to horse and dog racing. More and more companies are requiring their employees whose jobs involve dangerous work conditions or could impact the safety of others (such as truck drivers, airline pilots, and railroad workers) to undergo drug testing. This has meant more work for forensic toxicologists. This aspect of toxicology is usually confined to the detection of only a handful of specific drugs in a large number of urine samples—some laboratories perform tests on more than 10,000 samples a day. Testing of this type is evolving toward the use of specimens other than blood or urine, such as sweat, hair, and saliva.

Toxicologists carefully document their research procedures so that they can be used in later reports on their findings. They often interact with lawyers and legislators on writing legislation. They may also appear at official hearings designed to discuss and implement new policy decisions. Forensic toxicologists often testify in criminal proceedings.

Because toxic materials are often handled during research and experimentation, a toxicologist must pay careful attention to safety procedures.

# REQUIREMENTS

## High School
While in high school, you can best prepare for a career as a toxicologist by taking courses in both the physical and biological sciences (chemistry and biology, for example), algebra and geometry, and physics. English and other courses that improve written and verbal communication skills will also be useful, since toxicologists must write and report on complicated study results.

## Postsecondary Training
Most toxicologists obtain their undergraduate degrees in a scientific field, such as pharmacology or chemistry. Course work should include mathematics (including mathematical modeling), biology, chemistry, statistics, biochemistry, pathology, anatomy, and research methods.

Career opportunities for graduates with bachelor's degrees are limited; the majority of toxicologists go on to obtain master's or doctorate degrees in toxicology, pathology, molecular biology, or a related field. Doctorate programs generally last four to five years.

The Society of Toxicology offers a list of colleges and universities that offer educational programs in toxicology at its Web site, http://www.toxicology.org/ai/apt/careerprograms.asp.

## Certification or Licensing
Certification recognizes an individual's competence and expertise in toxicology and can enhance career opportunities. Voluntary certification is available from the American Board of Toxicology and the American Board of Forensic Toxicology. Contact these organizations for more information.

## Other Requirements
Toxicologists must be hard workers and be dedicated to their field of study. To succeed in their work, they must be careful observers and have an eye for detail. Patience is also necessary, since many research projects can last months to years and show little results. The ability to work both alone and as part of a team is also needed for research.

Because of the nature of their work, toxicologists must also realize the potential dangers of working with hazardous materials. They must also be comfortable working with laboratory animals and be able to dissect them to examine organs and tissues. Though efforts have been made to limit and control live animal experimentation, research still requires their use to identify toxins and, in turn, protect the consumer public.

## EXPLORING

If you are interested in pursuing a career as a toxicologist, consider joining a science club in addition to taking biology and chemistry courses to further develop your laboratory skills. Your career counselor might be able to help you arrange a discussion with a practicing toxicologist to explore career options. Part-time jobs in research laboratories or hospitals are an excellent way to explore science firsthand, although opportunities may be limited and require higher levels of education and experience.

## EMPLOYERS

A Society of Toxicology job market survey of those with Ph.D.'s shows that 35 percent work in industry (mainly for chemical and pharmaceutical companies), 21 percent are employed in academia, and 18 percent work in government. Others work for nonprofit research foundations and consulting firms, providing professional recommendations to agencies, industries, and attorneys about issues involving toxic chemicals.

## STARTING OUT

Those with the necessary education and experience should contact the appropriate research departments in hospitals, colleges and universities, government agencies, or private businesses. Often, school professors and career services advisers provide job leads and recommendations.

Networking with professionals is another useful way to enter the field. Past work with a team of toxicologists during graduate study may open doors to future research opportunities. Membership in a professional society can also offer more networking contacts. In addition, the Society of Toxicology and the American College of Medical Toxicology, and other organizations offer job placement assistance to members.

## ADVANCEMENT

Skilled toxicologists will find many advancement opportunities, although specific promotions depend on the size and type of organization where the toxicologist is employed. Those working for private companies may become heads of research departments. Because of their involvement in developing important company policy, highly skilled and respected toxicologists may become vice presidents or presidents of companies. Obviously, this type of promotion would entail a change in job responsibilities, involving more administrative tasks than research activities.

Toxicologists working for educational institutions may become professors, heads of a department, or deans. Toxicologists who want to continue to research and teach can advance to positions with higher pay and increased job responsibilities. Toxicologists working at universities usually write grant proposals, teach courses, and train graduate students. University positions often do not pay as well as industrial positions, but they offer more independence in pursuing research interests.

## EARNINGS

As trained professionals, toxicologists have good earning potential. Wages vary depending on level of experience, education, and employer. According to a survey by the Society of Toxicology, entry-level toxicologists with a Ph.D. earn $35,000 to $60,000. With a Ph.D. and 10 years of experience, toxicologists can earn between $70,000 and $100,000 a year. Toxicologists in executive positions earn more than $100,000, and in the corporate arena they can earn more than $200,000. Those in private industry earn slightly more than those in government or academic positions. Payscale.com lists toxicologist salaries in 2010 ranging from $54,627 to $113,402, and Salary.com lists a median salary of $68,592.

Salaries for toxicologists are, in general, on the rise, but the survey reports that the biggest factor determining earning potential is not location but type of employer. Certification also plays a large role in salary level; toxicologists who are certified earn higher salaries than those who have not earned certification. Comparing gender differences, the salary survey found that women continue to be paid less than their male counterparts.

Toxicologists who work for a company or government agency usually receive benefits such as vacation days, sick leave, health and life insurance, and a savings and pension program. Self-employed toxicologists must provide their own benefits.

## WORK ENVIRONMENT

Toxicologists usually work in well-equipped laboratories or offices, either as part of a team or alone. Research in libraries or in the field is a major part of the job. Some toxicologists work a standard 40-hour workweek, although many work longer hours. Overtime should be expected if an important research project is on deadline. Research and experimentation can be both physically and mentally tiring, with much of the laboratory work and analysis done while under time restrictions. Some travel may be required to testify at hearings, to collect field samples, or to attend professional conferences.

Toxicologists often work on research that has important health considerations. At a poison control center, for example, toxicologists may try to find information about the poisonous properties of a product while an overdose victim's life is in danger. Because their work involves studying the impact of toxic material, toxicologists must be willing to handle contaminated material and adhere to the strict safety precautions required.

## OUTLOOK

Employment opportunities for toxicologists are expected to continue to be good. The growing use of chemicals and pharmaceuticals by society has created demand for trained professionals to determine and limit the health risks associated with potential toxins. In addition, new concerns over bioterrorism and the potential use of chemical weapons will create more demand for toxicologists to help develop new vaccines and other antibiotics.

Job opportunities should be greatest in large urban areas where many large hospitals, chemical manufacturers, and university research facilities are located. Those with the most training and experience will have the best prospects in finding employment.

## FOR MORE INFORMATION

*For information on certification, contact*
American Board of Forensic Toxicology
410 North 21st Street
Colorado Springs, CO 80904-2712
Tel: 719-636-1100
http://www.abft.org

*For information on certification, contact*
**American Board of Toxicology**
PO Box 30054
Raleigh, NC 27622-0054
Tel: 919-841-5022
E-mail: info@abtox.org
http://www.abtox.org

*For information on educational programs and other toxicology resources, contact*
**American College of Medical Toxicology**
10645 North Tatum Boulevard, Suite 200-111
Phoenix, AZ 85028-3068
Tel: 623-533-6340
E-mail: info@acmt.net
http://www.acmt.net

*For information on toxicology, contact*
**American College of Toxicology**
9650 Rockville Pike
Bethesda, MD 20814-3999
Tel: 301-634-7840
http://www.actox.org

*For more information about forensic toxicology, contact*
**International Association of Forensic Toxicologists**
E-mail: info@tiaft.org
http://www.tiaft.org

*For industry information, contact*
**Society of Environmental Toxicology and Chemistry**
1010 North 12th Avenue
Pensacola, FL 32501-3370
Tel: 850-469-1500
E-mail: setac@setac.org
http://www.setac.org

*For information on forensic toxicology and career options in the field, contact*
**Society of Forensic Toxicologists**
One MacDonald Center
1 North MacDonald Street, Suite 15
Mesa, AZ 85201-7340

Tel: 888-866-7638
E-mail: office@soft-tox.org
http://www.soft-tox.org

*For general career information, contact*
**Society of Toxicology**
1821 Michael Faraday Drive, Suite 300
Reston, VA 20190-5348
Tel: 703-438-3115
E-mail: sothq@toxicology.org
http://www.toxicology.org

# Veterinarians

## OVERVIEW

The *veterinarian*, or *doctor of veterinary medicine*, diagnoses and controls animal diseases, treats sick and injured animals medically and surgically, prevents transmission of animal diseases, and advises owners on proper care of pets and livestock. Veterinarians are dedicated to the protection of the health and welfare of all animals and to society as a whole. There are about 59,700 veterinarians in the United States.

## HISTORY

The first school of veterinary medicine was opened in 1762 at Lyons, France. Nearly 100 years later, a French physician and veterinarian named Alexandre Francois Liautard immigrated to the United States and became a leader in the movement to establish veterinary medicine as a science. Through his efforts, an organization was started in 1863 that later became the American Veterinary Medical Association. Veterinary medicine has made great strides since its introduction in this country, one advance being the significant reduction in animal diseases contracted by humans.

## THE JOB

Veterinarians care for pets—large and small. They ensure a safe food supply by maintaining the health of food animals. They also protect the public from residues of herbicides, pesticides, and antibiotics in food. Veterinarians may be involved in wildlife preservation and conservation and use their knowledge to increase food production through genetics, animal feed production, and preventive medicine.

# Books to Read

McBride, Douglas F., and Miriam and Harvey Austrin. *Learning Veterinary Terminology.* 2d ed. St. Louis: Mosby, 2001.

Robinson, Phillip T. *Life at the Zoo: Behind the Scenes with the Animal Doctors.* New York: Columbia University Press, 2007.

Shenk, Ellen. *Careers With Animals: Exploring Occupations Involving Dogs, Horses, Cats, Birds, Wildlife, and Exotics.* Mechanicsburg, Pa.: Stackpole Books, 2005.

Spelman, Lucy H., and Ted Y. Mashima. *The Rhino with Glue-On Shoes: And Other Surprising True Stories of Zoo Vets and their Patients.* New York: Delacorte Press, 2008.

Stewart, Liz. *Vault Career Guide to Veterinary and Animal Careers.* New York: Vault Inc., 2008.

Trout, Nick. *Tell Me Where It Hurts: A Day of Humor, Healing and Hope in My Life as an Animal Surgeon.* New York: Broadway Books, 2009.

Wells, Jeff. *All My Patients Have Tales: Favorite Stories from a Vet's Practice.* New York: St. Martin's Press, 2009.

About 80 percent of veterinarians are employed in solo or group veterinary medicine practices. Although some veterinarians treat all kinds of animals, more than half limit their practice to companion animals such as dogs, cats, and birds. A smaller number of veterinarians work mainly with horses, cattle, pigs, sheep, goats, and poultry. Today, a veterinarian may treat llamas, catfish, or ostriches as well. Others are employed by wildlife management groups, zoos, aquariums, ranches, feedlots, fish farms, and animal shelters.

Veterinarians in private practice diagnose and treat animal health problems. During yearly checkups, the veterinarian records the animal's temperature and weight; inspects its mouth, eyes, and ears; inspects the skin or coat for any signs of abnormalities; observes any peculiarities in the animal's behavior; and discusses the animals eating, sleeping, and exercise habits at length with the owner. The veterinarian will also check the animal's vaccination records and administer inoculations for rabies, distemper, and other diseases if necessary. If the veterinarian or owner notes any special concerns, or if the animal is taken to the veterinarian for a specific procedure, such as spaying or neutering, dental cleaning, or setting broken bones, the animal may stay at the veterinarian's office for one or several days for surgery, observation, or extended treatments. If a sick or wounded animal is beyond medical help, the veterinarian may, with the consent of the owner, have to euthanize the animal.

During office visits and surgery, veterinarians use traditional medical instruments, such as stethoscopes, thermometers, and surgical instruments, and standard tests, such as X-rays and diagnostic medical sonography, to evaluate the animal's health. Veterinarians may also prescribe drugs for the animal, which the owner purchases at the veterinarian's office.

Some veterinarians work in public and corporate sectors. Many are employed by city, county, state, provincial, or federal government agencies that investigate, test for, and control diseases in companion animals, livestock, and poultry that affect both animal and human health. Veterinarians also play an important public health role. For example, veterinarians played an important part in conquering diseases such as malaria and yellow fever.

Pharmaceutical and biomedical research firms hire veterinarians to develop, test, and supervise the production of drugs, chemicals, and biological products such as antibiotics and vaccines that are designed for human and animal use. Some veterinarians are employed in management, technical sales and services, and marketing in agribusiness, pet food companies, and pharmaceutical companies. Still other veterinarians are engaged in research and teaching at veterinary medical schools, working with racetracks or animal-related enterprises, or working within the military, public health corps, and space agencies.

The U.S. Department of Agriculture has opportunities for veterinarians in the Food Safety and Inspection Service and the Animal and Plant Health Inspection Service, notably in the areas of food hygiene and safety, animal welfare, animal disease control, and research. Veterinarians also are employed by the Environmental Protection Agency to deal with public health and environmental risks to the human population.

Veterinarians are often assisted by *veterinary technicians* and *technologists*, who may conduct basic tests, record an animal's medical history for the veterinarian's review, and assist the veterinarian in surgical procedures.

## REQUIREMENTS

### High School

For the high school student who is interested in admission to a school of veterinary medicine, a college preparatory course is a wise choice.

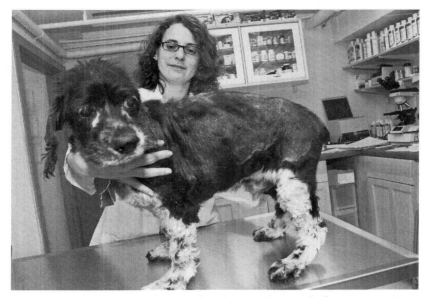

A veterinarian who specializes in dog dermatology and allergies examines a cocker spaniel with severe skin allergies. *(Michael Sofronski, The Image Works)*

A strong emphasis on science classes such as biology, chemistry, and anatomy is highly recommended.

## Postsecondary Training

The doctor of veterinary medicine (D.V.M.) degree requires a minimum of four years of study at an accredited college of veterinary medicine. Although many of these colleges do not require a bachelor's degree for admission, most require applicants to have completed 45–90 hours of undergraduate study. It is possible to obtain preveterinary training at a junior college, but since admission to colleges of veterinary medicine is an extremely competitive process, most students receive degrees from four-year colleges before applying. In addition to academic instruction, veterinary education includes clinical experience in diagnosing disease and treating animals, performing surgery, and performing laboratory work in anatomy, biochemistry, and other scientific and medical subjects.

There are 28 colleges of veterinary medicine in the United States that are accredited by the Council of Veterinary Medicine of the American Veterinary Medical Association (AVMA). Each college of veterinary medicine has its own preveterinary requirements, which typically include basic language arts, social sciences, humanities, mathematics, chemistry, and biological and physical sciences. Veterinarians in private clinical practice become specialists in surgery, anesthesiology, dentistry, internal medicine, ophthalmology, or radiology. Many veterinarians also pursue advanced degrees in the basic sciences, such as anatomy, microbiology, and physiology.

Applicants to schools of veterinary medicine usually must have grades of "B" or better, especially in the sciences. Applicants must take the Veterinary College Admission Test, Medical College Admission Test, or the Graduate Record Examination. Only about one-third of applicants to schools of veterinary medicine are admitted, due to small class sizes and limited facilities. Most colleges give preference to candidates with animal- or veterinary-related experience. Colleges usually give preference to in-state applicants because most colleges of veterinary medicine are state-supported. There are regional agreements in which states without veterinary schools send students to designated regional schools.

Veterinary medicine students typically participate in one or more internships during their college careers. The internships allow them to learn more about career options in the field and make valuable industry contacts.

### Certification or Licensing

Veterinarians who seek specialty board certification in one of nearly 40 specialty fields must complete a two- to five-year residency program and pass an additional examination. Some veterinarians combine their degree in veterinary medicine with a degree in business or law. Contact the AVMA American Board of Veterinary Specialties (http://www.avma.org/education/abvs) for more information.

All states and the District of Columbia require that veterinarians be licensed to practice private clinical medicine. To obtain a license, applicants must have a D.V.M. degree from an accredited or approved college of veterinary medicine. They must also pass one or more national examinations and an examination in the state in which they plan to practice.

Few states issue licenses to veterinarians already licensed by another state. Thus, if a veterinarian moves from one state to another, he or she will probably have to go through the licensing process again. Nearly all states require veterinarians to attend continuing education courses in order to maintain their licenses. Veterinarians may be employed by a government agency (such as the U.S. Department of Agriculture) or by some academic institutions without having a state license.

## Other Requirements

Individuals who are interested in veterinary medicine should have an inquiring mind and keen powers of observation. Aptitude and interest in the biological sciences are important. Veterinarians need a lifelong interest in scientific learning as well as a liking and understanding of animals. Veterinarians should be able to meet, talk, and work well with a variety of people. An ability to communicate with the animal owner is as important in a veterinarian as diagnostic skills.

Veterinarians use state-of-the-art medical equipment, such as electron microscopes, laser surgery, radiation therapy, and ultrasound, to diagnose animal diseases and to treat sick or injured animals. Although manual dexterity and physical stamina are often required, especially for farm vets, important roles in veterinary medicine can be adapted for those with disabilities.

Interaction with animal owners is a very important part of being a veterinarian. The discussions between vet and owner are critical to the veterinarian's diagnosis, so he or she must be able to communicate effectively and get along with a wide variety of personalities. Veterinarians may have to euthanize (that is, humanely kill) an animal that is very sick or severely injured and cannot get well. When a beloved pet dies, the veterinarian must deal with the owner's grief and loss.

## EXPLORING

High school students interested in becoming veterinarians may find part-time or volunteer work on farms, in small-animal clinics, or in pet shops, animal shelters, or research laboratories. Participation in extracurricular activities such as 4-H are good ways to learn about the care of animals. Such experience is important because, as already noted, many schools of veterinary medicine have established experience with animals as a criterion for admission to their programs. Other methods of exploration include talking to a veterinarian about his or her career, reading books and magazines about veterinary science, and visiting the Web sites of veterinary associations and veterinary medical colleges.

## EMPLOYERS

Approximately 59,700 veterinarians are employed in the United States. Veterinarians may work for schools and universities, wildlife management groups, zoos, aquariums, ranches, feedlots, fish farms, pet food or pharmaceutical companies, and the government (mainly in the U.S. Departments of Agriculture and the U.S. Food and Drug

Administration's Center for Veterinary Medicine, but also for the Department of Homeland Security). The vast majority, however, are employed by veterinary clinical practices or hospitals. Many successful veterinarians in private practice are self-employed and may even employ other veterinarians. An increase in the demand for veterinarians is anticipated, particularly for those who specialize in areas related to public health issues such as food safety and disease control. Cities and large metropolitan areas will probably provide the bulk of new jobs for these specialists, while jobs for veterinarians who specialize in large animals will be focused in remote, rural areas.

## STARTING OUT

The only way to become a veterinarian is through the prescribed degree program, and vet schools are set up to assist their graduates in finding employment. Veterinarians who wish to enter private clinical practice must have a license to practice in their particular state before opening an office. Licenses are obtained by passing the state's examination.

Information about employment opportunities can be obtained by contacting employers directly or through career services offices of veterinary medicine colleges. Additionally, professional associations such as the American Association of Zoo Veterinarians, the American Association of Wildlife Veterinarians, the Association of American Veterinary Medical Colleges, and the American Veterinary Medical Association offer job listings at their Web sites.

## ADVANCEMENT

New graduate veterinarians may enter private clinical practice, usually as employees in an established practice, or become employees of the U.S. government as meat and poultry inspectors, disease control workers, and commissioned officers in the U.S. Public Health Service or the military. New graduates may also enter internships and residencies at veterinary colleges and large private and public veterinary practices or become employed by industrial firms.

The veterinarian who is employed by a government agency may advance in grade and salary after accumulating time and experience on the job. For the veterinarian in private clinical practice, advancement usually consists of an expanding practice and the higher income that will result from it or becoming an owner of several practices.

Those who teach or do research may obtain a doctorate and move from the rank of instructor to that of full professor, or they may advance to an administrative position.

# EARNINGS

The U.S. Department of Labor (DOL) reports that median annual earnings of veterinarians were $80,510 in 2009. Salaries ranged from less than $47,670 to more than $142,910. The mean annual salary for veterinarians working for the federal government was $84,200 in 2009.

The average starting salary for veterinary medical college graduates who worked exclusively with small animals was $69,154 in 2009, according to a survey by the American Veterinary Medical Association. Those who worked exclusively with large animals earned an average of $63,172. Equine veterinarians earned an average of $37,854 to start. The average starting salary for all veterinarians was $48,684.

Benefits include paid vacation, health, disability, life insurance, and retirement or pension plans. Self-employed veterinarians must provide their own benefits.

# WORK ENVIRONMENT

Veterinarians usually treat companion and food animals in hospitals and clinics. Those in large animal practice also work out of well-equipped trucks or cars and may drive considerable distances to farms and ranches. They may work outdoors in all kinds of weather. The chief risk for veterinarians is injury by animals; however, modern tranquilizers and technology have made it much easier to work on all types of animals.

Most veterinarians work long hours, often 50 or more hours a week. Although those in private clinical practice may work nights and weekends, the increased number of emergency clinics has reduced the amount of time private practitioners have to be on call. Large animal practitioners tend to work more irregular hours than those in small animal practice, industry, or government. Veterinarians who are just starting a practice tend to work longer hours.

# OUTLOOK

Employment of veterinarians is expected to grow much faster than the average for all careers through 2018, according to the DOL. The number of pets (especially cats) is expected to increase because of rising incomes and an increase in the number of people aged 34 to 59, among whom pet ownership has historically been the highest. Approximately 63 percent of U.S. households owned a pet in 2008, according to the American Pet Products Association. Many single adults and senior citizens have come to appreciate animal ownership.

Pet owners also may be willing to pay for more elective and intensive care than in the past. In addition, emphasis on scientific methods of breeding and raising livestock, poultry, and fish, and continued support for public health and disease control programs will contribute to the demand for veterinarians.

The outlook is good for veterinarians with specialty training. Demand for specialists in toxicology, laboratory animal medicine, and pathology is expected to increase. Most jobs for specialists will be in metropolitan areas. Prospects for veterinarians who concentrate on environmental and public health issues, aquaculture, and food animal practice appear to be excellent because of perceived increased need in these areas. Positions in small animal specialties will be competitive. Opportunities in farm animal specialties will be excellent because most of these positions are located in remote, rural areas, where many veterinarians do not want to practice.

## FOR MORE INFORMATION

*For career information, contact*
**Academy of Rural Veterinarians**
1450 Western Avenue, Suite 101
Albany, NY 12203-3539
Tel: 518-694-0056
E-mail: arv@caphill.com
http://www.ruralvets.com

*For information on equine veterinary science, contact*
**American Association of Equine Practitioners**
4075 Iron Works Parkway
Lexington, KY 40511-8483
Tel: 859-233-0147
E-mail: aaepoffice@aaep.org
http://www.aaep.org

*Visit the association's Web site for job listings and information about wildlife veterinarians.*
**American Association of Wildlife Veterinarians**
http://www.aawv.net

*Visit the association's Web site for job listings, news about zoos around the world, the* Journal of Zoo & Wildlife Medicine, *information on internships and externships and zoo and wildlife clubs for veterinary students, and discussion boards.*

American Association of Zoo Veterinarians
581705 White Oak Road
Yulee, FL 32097-2169
Tel: 904-225-3275
E-mail: aazvorg@aol.com
http://www.aazv.org

*For information on animal behavior, visit*
American College of Veterinary Behaviorists
http://www.dacvb.org

*For more information on careers, schools, and resources, contact*
American Veterinary Medical Association
1931 North Meacham Road, Suite 100
Schaumburg, IL 60173-4360
Tel: 800-248-2862
E-mail: avmainfo@avma.org
http://www.avma.org

*For information on veterinary opportunities in the federal government, contact*
Animal and Plant Health Inspection Service
1400 Independence Avenue, SW
Washington, DC 20250-0002
E-mail: VS_Content_Management@aphis.usda.gov
http://www.aphis.usda.gov

*For information educational programs, contact*
Association of American Veterinary Medical Colleges
1101 Vermont Avenue, NW, Suite 301
Washington, DC 20005-3539
Tel: 202-371-9195
http://www.aavmc.org

*For information on education and internships, contact*
International Association of Aquatic Animal Medicine
E-mail: fmb@resoundinternational.org.uk
http://www.iaaam.org

*For information on veterinary careers in Canada, contact*
Canadian Veterinary Medical Association
339 Booth Street
Ottawa, ON K1R 7K1 Canada
Tel: 613-236-1162
E-mail: admin@cvma-acmv.org
http://www.canadianveterinarians.net

# Zoologists

## OVERVIEW

*Zoologists* are biologists who study animals. They often select a particular type of animal to study, and they may study an entire animal, one part or aspect of an animal, or a whole animal society. There are many areas of specialization from which a zoologist can choose, such as origins, genetics, characteristics, classifications, behaviors, life processes, and distribution of animals.

## HISTORY

Human beings have always studied animals. Knowledge of animal behavior was a necessity to prehistoric humans, whose survival depended on their success in hunting. Those early people who hunted to live learned to respect and even revere their prey. The earliest known paintings, located in the Lascaux Caves in France, depict animals, which demonstrates the importance of animals to early humans. Most experts believe that the artists who painted those images viewed the animals they hunted not just as a food source, but also as an important element of spiritual or religious life.

The first important developments in zoology occurred in Greece, where Alcmaeon, a philosopher and physician, studied animals and performed the first known dissections of humans in the sixth century B.C. Aristotle, however, is generally considered to be the first real zoologist. Aristotle, who studied with the great philosopher Plato and tutored the world-conquering Alexander the Great, had the lofty goal of setting down in writing everything that was known in his time. In an attempt to extend that knowledge, he observed and dissected sea creatures. He also devised a system of classifying animals that included 500 species, a system that influenced scientists for many centuries after his death. Some scholars believe that Alexander sent various exotic animals to his old tutor from the lands he conquered, giving Aristotle unparalleled access to the animals of the ancient world.

With the exception of important work in physiology done by the Roman physician Galen, the study of zoology progressed little after Aristotle until the middle of the 16th century. Between 1555 and 1700, much significant work was done in the classification of species and in physiology, especially regarding the circulation of blood, which affected studies of both animals and humans. The invention of the microscope in approximately 1590 led to the discovery and study of cells. In the 18th century, Swedish botanist Carl Linnaeus developed the system of classification of plants and animals that is still used.

Zoology continued to develop at a rapid rate, and in 1859, Charles Darwin published *On the Origin of Species*, which promoted the theory of natural selection, revolutionized the way scientists viewed all living creatures, and gave rise to the field of ethology, the study of animal behavior. Since that time, innumerable advances have been made by zoologists throughout the world.

## On the Web

Animal Corner
http://www.animalcorner.co.uk

Animal Diversity Web
http://animaldiversity.ummz.umich.edu

Animal Fact Guide
http://www.animalfactguide.com

Animal Planet
http://animal.discovery.com

Insectclopedia
http://www.insectclopedia.com

Oakland Zoo: Animals
http://www.oaklandzoo.org/animals

SeaWorld: Animals
http://www.seaworld.org

In the past century, the rapid development of technology has changed zoology and all sciences by giving scientists the tools to explore areas that had previously been closed to them. Computers, submersibles, high-definition cameras, geographic information systems technology, satellites, and tremendously powerful microscopes are only a few of the means that modern zoologists have used to bring new knowledge to light. In spite of these advances, however, mysteries remain, questions go unanswered, and species wait to be discovered.

## THE JOB

Although zoology is a single specialty within the field of biology, it is a vast specialty that includes many major subspecialties. Some zoologists study a single animal or a category of animals, whereas others may specialize in a particular part of an animal's anatomy or study a process that takes place in many kinds of animals. A zoologist might study single-cell organisms, a particular variety of fish, or the behavior of groups of animals such as whales or seals.

Many zoologists are classified according to the animals they study. For example, *entomologists* are experts on insects, *ichthyologists* study fish, *herpetologists* specialize in the study of reptiles and amphibians, *mammalogists* focus on mammals, and *ornithologists* study birds. *Embryologists*, however, are classified according to the process that they study. They examine the ways in which animal embryos form and develop from conception to birth.

Within each primary area of specialization there is a wide range of subspecialties. An ichthyologist, for example, might focus on the physiology, or physical structure and functioning, of a particular fish; on a biochemical phenomenon such as bioluminescence in deep-sea species; on the discovery and classification of fish; on variations within a single species in different parts of the world; or on the ways in which one type of fish interacts with other species in a specific environment. Others may specialize in the effects of pollution on fish or in finding ways to grow fish effectively in controlled environments in order to increase the supply of healthy food available for human consumption.

Some zoologists are primarily teachers, while others spend most of their time performing original research. Teaching jobs in universities and other facilities are probably the most secure positions available, but zoologists who wish to do extensive research may find such positions restrictive. Even zoologists whose primary function is research, however, often need to do some teaching in the course of their work, and almost everyone in the field has to deal with the public at one time or another.

Students often believe that zoological scientists spend most of their time in the field, observing animals and collecting specimens. In fact, most researchers spend no more than two to eight weeks in the field each year. Zoologists spend much of their time at a computer or on the telephone.

It is often the case that junior scientists spend more time in the field than do senior scientists, who study specimens and data collected in the field by their younger colleagues. Senior scientists spend much of their time coordinating research, directing younger scientists and technicians, and writing grant proposals or soliciting funds in other ways.

Raising money is an extremely important activity for zoologists who are not employed by government agencies or major universities. The process of obtaining money for research can be time-consuming and difficult. Good development skills can also give scientists a flexibility that government-funded scientists do not have. Government money is sometimes available only for research in narrowly defined areas that may not be those that a scientist wishes to study. A zoologist who wants to study a particular area may seek his or her own funding in order not to be limited by government restrictions.

## REQUIREMENTS

### High School

To prepare for a career in zoology, make sure to get a well-rounded high school education. Although a solid grounding in biology and chemistry is an absolute necessity, you should remember that facility in English will also be invaluable. Writing monographs and articles, communicating with colleagues both orally and in writing, and writing persuasive fund-raising proposals are all activities at which scientists need to excel. You should also read widely, not merely relying on books on science or other subjects that are required by the school. The scientist-in-training should search the library for magazines and journals dealing with areas that are of personal interest. Developing the habit of reading will help prepare you for the massive amounts of reading involved in research and keeping up with latest developments in the field. Computer skills are also essential, since most zoologists not only use the computer for writing, communication, and research, but they also use various software programs to perform statistical analyses.

An ornithologist examines a white stork nestling after counting the growth in the nest during the annual stork tracking program in Gomba, Hungary. *(Bela Szandelszky, AP Photo)*

## Postsecondary Training

A bachelor's degree is the minimum requirement to work as a zoologist; advanced degrees are needed for research or administrative work. Academic training, practical experience, and the ability to work effectively with others are the most important prerequisites for a career in zoology.

## Other Requirements

Success in zoology requires tremendous effort. It would be unwise for a person who wants to work an eight-hour day to become a zoologist, since hard work and long hours (sometimes 60 to 80 hours per week) are the norm. Also, although some top scientists are paid extremely well, the field does not provide a rapid route to riches. A successful zoologist finds satisfaction in work, not in a paycheck. The personal rewards, however, can be tremendous. The typical zoologist finds his or her work satisfying on many levels.

A successful zoologist is generally patient and flexible. A person who cannot juggle various tasks will have a difficult time in a job that requires doing research, writing articles, dealing with the public, teaching students, soliciting funds, and keeping up with the latest publications in the field. Flexibility also comes into play when funding for a particular area of study ends or is unavailable. A zoologist whose range of expertise is too narrowly focused will be at a disadvantage when there are no opportunities in that particular area. A flexible approach and a willingness to explore various areas can be crucial in such situations, and a too-rigid attitude may lead a zoologist to avoid studies that he or she would have found rewarding.

An aptitude for reading and writing is a must for any zoologist. A person who hates to read would have difficulty keeping up with the literature in the field, and a person who cannot write or dislikes writing would be unable to write effective articles and books. Publishing is an important part of zoological work, especially for those who are conducting research.

## EXPLORING

One of the best ways to find out if you are suited for a career as a zoologist is to talk to zoologists and find out exactly what they do. Contact experts in your field of interest. If you are interested in birds, find out whether there is an ornithologist in your area. If there is not, find an expert in some other part of the country. Read books, magazines, and journals to find out whom the experts are. Don't be afraid to write or call people and ask them questions.

One good way to meet experts is to attend meetings of professional organizations. If you are interested in fish, locate organizations of ichthyologists by searching in the library or on the Internet. If you can, attend an organization's meeting and introduce yourself to the attendees. Ask questions and learn as much as you can.

Try to become an intern or a volunteer at an organization that is involved in an area that you find interesting. Most organizations have internships, and if you look with determination for an internship, you are likely to find one.

## EMPLOYERS

Zoologists are employed by a wide variety of institutions, not just zoos. Many zoologists are teachers at universities and other facilities, where they may teach during the year while spending their summers doing research. A large number of zoologists are researchers; they may be working for nonprofit organizations (requiring grants to fund their work), scientific institutions, or the government. Of course, there are many zoologists who are employed by zoos, aquariums, and museums. While jobs for zoologists exist all over the country, large cities that have universities, zoos, aquariums, and museums will provide far more opportunities for zoologists than in rural areas.

## STARTING OUT

Though it is possible to find work with a bachelor's degree, it is likely that you will need to continue your education to advance further in the field. Competition for higher paying, high-level jobs among those with doctoral degrees is fierce; as a result, it is often easier to break into the field with a master's degree than it is with a Ph.D. Many zoologists with their master's degree seek a mid-level job and work toward a Ph.D. part time.

You will be ahead of the game if you have made contacts as an intern or as a member of a professional organization. It is an excellent idea to attend the meetings of professional organizations, which generally welcome students. At those meetings, introduce yourself to the scientists you admire and ask for their help and advice. Don't be shy, but be sure to treat people with respect. Ultimately, it's the way you relate to other people that determines how your career will develop.

## ADVANCEMENT

Higher education and publishing are two of the most important means of advancing in the field of zoology. The holder of a Ph.D. will make more money and have a higher status than the holder of a bachelor's or master's degree. The publication of articles and books is important for both research scientists and professors of zoology. A young professor who does not publish cannot expect to become a full professor with tenure, and a research scientist who does not publish the results of his or her research will not become known as an authority in the field. In addition, the publication of a significant work lets everyone in the field know that the author has worked hard and accomplished something worthwhile.

Because zoology is not a career in which people typically move from job to job, people generally move up within an organization. A professor may become a full professor; a research scientist may become known as an expert in the field or may become the head of a department, division, or institution; a zoologist employed by an aquarium or a zoo may become an administrator or head curator. In some cases, however, scientists may not want what appears to be a more prestigious position. A zoologist who loves to conduct and coordinate research, for example, may not want to become an administrator who is responsible for budgeting, hiring and firing, and other tasks that have nothing to do with research.

## EARNINGS

A July 2009 survey conducted by the National Association of Colleges and Employers determined that holders of bachelor's degrees in biological and life sciences (including zoologists) earned average starting salaries of $33,254.

The median annual wage for zoologists in 2009 was $56,500, according to the U.S. Department of Labor (DOL). Salaries ranged from less than $35,280 to $93,140 or more. Zoologists who were employed by the federal government had mean annual earnings of $116,908.

It is possible for the best and brightest of zoologists to make substantial amounts of money. Occasionally, a newly graduated Ph.D. who has a top reputation may be offered a position that pays $100,000 or more per year, but only a few people begin their careers at such a high level.

The benefits that zoologists receive as part of their employment vary widely. Employees of the federal government or top universities tend to have extensive benefit packages, but the benefits offered by private industry cover a wide range, from extremely generous to almost nonexistent.

## WORK ENVIRONMENT

There is much variation in the conditions under which zoologists work. Professors of zoology may teach exclusively during the school year or may both teach and conduct research. Many professors whose school year consists of teaching spend their summers doing research. Research scientists spend some time in the field, but most of their work is done in the laboratory. There are zoologists who spend most of their time in the field, but they are the exceptions to the rule.

Zoologists who do field work may have to deal with difficult conditions. For example, a gorilla expert may have to spend her time in the forests of Rwanda. A shark expert may need to observe his subjects from a shark cage. A marine ornithologist may have to walk the craggy shoreline during brisk weather to observe birds. For most people in the field, however, that aspect of the work is particularly interesting and satisfying.

Zoologists spend much of their time corresponding with others in their field, studying the latest literature, reviewing articles written by their peers, and making and returning phone calls. They also log many hours working with computers, using computer modeling, performing statistical analyses, recording the results of their research, or writing articles and grant proposals.

No zoologist works in a vacuum. Even those who spend much time in the field have to keep up with developments within their specialty. In most cases, zoologists deal with many different kinds of people, including students, mentors, the public, colleagues, representatives of granting agencies, private or corporate donors, reporters, and science writers. For this reason, the most successful members of the profession tend to develop good communication skills.

## OUTLOOK

Employment for zoologists is expected to grow about as fast as the average for all careers through 2018, according to the DOL. The field of zoology is relatively small, and competition for good positions—especially research positions—is high. High-level jobs are further limited by government budget cuts. Growth in the biological sciences should continue in the next decade, spurred partly by the need to analyze and offset the effects of pollution on the environment. Competition will be strongest for those with doctoral degrees. Those with a bachelor's or master's degree will face less competition due to a larger number of available positions—including those in nonscientist jobs related to zoology, such as marketing, sales, publishing, and research management. Those who are most successful in the field in the future are likely to be those who are able to diversify. Zoologists with expertise in a variety of animals or animal systems or processes will have strong employment prospects.

## FOR MORE INFORMATION

*Visit the alliance's Web site for information on marine mammals, internships, and publications.*
**Alliance of Marine Mammal Parks and Aquariums**
E-mail: ammpa@aol.com
http://www.ammpa.org

*The Education section of the institute's Web site has information on a number of careers in biology.*
**American Institute of Biological Sciences**
1444 I Street, NW, Suite 200

Washington, DC 20005-6535
Tel: 202-628-1500
http://www.aibs.org

*For information on membership, a list of accredited zoos through-out the world, and careers in aquatic and marine science, including job listings, contact*
**Association of Zoos and Aquariums**
8403 Colesville Road, Suite 710
Silver Spring, MD 20910-3314
Tel: 301-562-0777
http://www.aza.org

*The society publishes the journal* Integrative and Comparative Biol-ogy, *and it is a good source of information about all areas and aspects of zoology. For more information, contact*
**Society for Integrative and Comparative Biology**
1313 Dolley Madison Boulevard, Suite 402
McLean, VA 22101-3926
Tel: 800-955-1236
E-mail: SICB@BurkInc.com
http://www.sicb.org

*The association "promotes conservation, preservation, and propa-gation of animals in both private and public domains." It offers a membership category for those who support its goals.*
**Zoological Association of America**
PO Box 511275
Punta Gorda, FL 33951-1275
Tel: 941-621-2021
E-mail: info@zaa.org
http://www.zaa.org

# Index